BISHOPS ON THE BIBLE

John V. Taylor is a former Bishop of Winchester (1975–85); his books include *The Go-Between God* (1972) and *Kingdom Come* (1989). Alec Graham is Bishop of Newcastle where he has been since 1981. He has been Chairman of the Doctrine Commission since 1987. Peter Selby was Suffragan Bishop of Kingston-upon-Thames from 1984 to 1992; he is now the William Leech Professorial Fellow in Applied Christian Theology in the University of Durham. He has written *Look for the Living* (1976), *Liberating God* (1983) and *BeLonging* (1991). David Jenkins has been Bishop of Durham since 1984. His publications include *Still Living With Questions* (1990) and *Free to Believe* (1991). David Hope was made Bishop of London in 1991. Philip Goodrich is Bishop of Worcester where he has been since 1982. Hugh Montefiore is a former Bishop of Birmingham (1978–87). His books include the popular *Confirmation Notebook*. John Oliver is Bishop of Hereford where he has been since 1990 and he is the author of *The Church and Social Order* (1968).

F4401

BISHOPS
on the
BIBLE

EIGHT BISHOPS ON THE ROLE AND RELEVANCE OF THE BIBLE TODAY

John V. Taylor, Alec Graham,
Peter Selby, David Jenkins,
David Hope, Philip Goodrich,
Hugh Montefiore, John Oliver

TRIANGLE

First published 1994
Triangle
SPCK
Holy Trinity Church
Marylebone Road
London NW1 4DU

British Library Cataloguing in Publication Data
A catalogue record for this book is available from the British Library.
ISBN 0-281-04708-1

Typeset by Inforum, Rowlands Castle, Hants
Printed and bound in Great Britain by
BPCC Paperbacks Ltd
Member of BPCC Ltd

CONTENTS

PREFACE

by the

Revd Canon Iain MacKenzie

This book contains the substance of a series of lectures delivered at St Giles-in-the-Fields, London, in October and November 1992.

The annual lecture courses were begun when the St Giles-in-the-Fields' school building was sold in 1970 by the diocese of London. By special arrangement with the diocese the Revd Gordon Taylor, now in his forty-fifth year as Rector, with great perspicacity established an educational trust for 'religious instruction' with part of the proceeds.

The purpose of the series of annual lectures established by this trust – 'The St Giles-in-the-Fields' Annual Bible School' – was to concentrate on the theological teaching of the Bible and its application. The first series was delivered in 1971 by the Revd Dr William Neil, who remained lecturer for several years. Since their inception, each series of lectures has made a successful and influential contribution to the educational work of the Church in London, having drawn since 1971 over 27,000 attendances. This reveals the thirst that exists for the opportunity of such instruction. Those attending the lectures are from many Christian denominations and come not only from central and greater London, but from the wider area of the surrounding counties and even farther afield.

Gordon Taylor is to be congratulated for his foresight and the determining of priorities. He had made available an invaluable theological resource, free of charge to those who attend, where the teaching given seeks to cover the competence of the searcher making his or her first steps in theological exploration, and yet also to satisfy the rigorous demands of the more academic world.

What is published here is the series given by eight bishops of the Church of England. The Rector of St Giles-in-the-Fields and I – and indeed the record number of people who attended in 1992 – are grateful to those bishops who willingly and readily gave their time and thought in delivering these lectures. I hope that the readers of this book likewise will benefit gratefully from the bishops' contributions.

Bishops are more-than-busy people with diaries well filled in advance. Some who were invited were unable to accept. The plan was to have a number of bishops whose contributions would reflect the comprehensive nature of the Church of England in their theological positions. We hope that this publication of the work of those able to accept conveys a sense of that comprehensiveness.

The contributors were invited to speak on the theme 'How I regard and use Holy Scripture'. No stricture was laid upon them except that they tackle the subject from their own standpoint with their own particular expertise and specific insights. The title of each lecture under the title of the general theme was left to the choice of the individual bishop.

I have to thank the bishops, who in the course of the complicated business in which I was engaged of finding dates convenient for everyone, arranged and in some cases re-arranged their diaries, when under the pressures endured by holders of the episcopal office, dates tentatively made had to be changed. Their understanding and generosity of mind made my task as acting Registrar for the St Giles' lectures so much easier.

We must also thank SPCK's theological editors for making the 1992 Annual Lectures of the St Giles-in-the-Fields' Bible School available to a wider audience by this publication.

Iain M. MacKenzie
Acting Registrar of St Giles-in-the-Fields

1

DIVINE REVELATION
THROUGH HUMAN EXPERIENCE
John V. Taylor

On being asked to contribute to a series of lectures on the theme of 'How I regard and use Holy Scripture?' I was thrown into a quandary. How *do* I regard and use Holy Scripture? When I affirm, as I do, that the Bible reveals authoritatively the nature and the purpose of God, what experience of using the Bible am I referring to? When I claim that the Scriptures afford divine guidance, not only for my own journey, but for the Church in the world, and even for human society, what experiences, and whose experiences, do I have in mind?

I had the good fortune to grow up among people who believed that the Bible is for amateurs and even children. Books of Bible stories were included in my childhood reading. The names of the outlaw David's merry men were as familiar to me as those of Robin Hood, and Balaam's dolorous ass belonged to the same stable as Eeyore. This detailed and largely unbowdlerised familiarity with the Bible as a book of good yarns gave me the inestimable benefit of knowing initially that, whatever else the Scriptures may contain, they consist essentially of things that happened, and of the people to whom and through whom they happened. This is the absolutely basic fact about these Jewish and Christian writings which distinguishes them from the scriptures of other faiths. Those who approach our Scriptures expecting a catalogue of doctrines necessary for salvation, or a code of moral conduct exemplified in the lives of holy men and women, may be quickly baffled because they have not realised that saving truths and guiding principles are mediated through the experience of events and people's subsequent reflection upon those experiences.

As I entered pre-adolescence I was introduced to a more self-absorbed use of Scripture. From the Evangelical tradition in which I was nurtured, I took on board, albeit in a desultory, stop-go fashion, the habit of reading a few verses of the Bible as the mainstay of my daily prayer time. I learned to look for an immediately personal application of what I was reading, so that Scripture became for me an anthology of memorable texts from among which I concentrated on those which brought me comfort or reproof, assurance, insight or inspiration. I began to experience the Bible as a Word from God addressed to my condition. That was the positive value of the little devotional books I was using, and was an absolutely necessary advance. But this pillaging of verses, sometimes with scant regard for the original context, and their arbitrary arrangement to endorse a chosen theme, gave me a falsely homogeneous picture of the Bible as a single, coherent book, serving and articulating one single message. It was as though an orchestral conductor had ordered all the instruments to play the successive themes of a Brahms symphony in unison, on the grounds that these were the melodies which the composer intended people to hear.

It was reading English and history at Cambridge that corrected this. I began to appreciate the relation between the meaning of any piece of literature and the historical situation within which it was written. I learned to guess at the period, and even the author, of an unidentified passage of prose or poetry from its style. I could tell myth from epic, romance from scholarly chronicle, a spontaneous report from a well-worn anecdote, and both from a literary narrative. Instinctively I could recognise all these, and many other kinds of writing, in the Old and New Testaments; and I wanted to read them as such, as myth or epic or song or history or sermon, if that was their nature. For I felt that that was how God had intended them to be the vehicle of his voice.

As I went on to take a degree in theology I discovered the prophets of Israel. Up till then they had merely contributed some purple passages to my anthology of personal comfort, reproof and doctrine. Now I was exhilarated by the distinct individualities that emerged from their recorded outbursts, their heroic protests against social wrongs, political follies, religious apostasy, their daring vision of a suffering, passionate God. I felt like someone well stocked with Shakespearean tags, who had just emerged, for the first time in his life, from a performance of one of Shakespeare's plays.

So I was ready, with very little loss of nerve or shaking of faith, to grasp the composite nature of many of the books of the Old Testament and of the Gospels; to value as an already familiar tool the so-called 'form criticism' or identification of certain stereotypes and conventions of languages demanded by different situations; and to try to discern from the texts themselves, and from other external evidence, the probable circumstances which any passage of Scripture was intended to address. And, while I have never aspired to more than amateur status in the realm of biblical studies, I have had the temerity to remain unconvinced by the findings of experts if they betray a *habitual* preference for the more extreme among possible conclusions.

I hope I am being honest when I say that, since those days, the Bible has been the principal means of communication in a lifelong relationship with God, though I must admit that, on my side, it has been an up-and-down relationship. The most adequate simile I can find for it is the mutual communication of a prolonged, though irregular, exchange of letters. One brings one's own thoughts and expectations to the study of a passage of Scripture, yet reflection upon it rarely endorses those ideas. So long as one brings a modicum of curiosity to it, the Bible literature almost always springs a surprise and presents something previously unnoticed, and not always welcome.

The exploration of a passage is, I find, best undertaken with, as it were, two maps of the area, one small-scale, one large. The small-scale map will show how the selected verses or chapters lie in relation to what immediately precedes and follows, and in relation to the story or the book as a whole. This is where the critical questions contribute so greatly. What sort of writing or speaking is this? For whom was it written and for what situation? What was the writer/speaker hoping to achieve? The large-scale map, on the other hand, directs attention to the details of the text itself – the words that have been chosen, and perhaps repeated; the order in which things are told; the tenses that have been used; the things which, surprisingly, are *not* said. Though I cannot read Hebrew and my Greek is rusty, I find endless illumination from the use of two well-worn tools: Robert Young's *Analytical Concordance to the Bible*, and Edward Robinson's *Greek and English Lexicon of the New Testament*[1]. With their aid, and with no more searching than any philatelist or birdwatcher would gladly undertake, I can find new slants of meaning, rich associations with other parts of the Bible, and hallmarks characteristic of a particular author.

So, until recently when the term became discredited, I would describe my theology as biblical theology because, as a definition, this must patently imply an ever-unfolding perception of the significance of certain crucial events. From the way in which Scripture actually 'works', actually speaks to our human condition in our own time, I derive all the meaning I can give to such words as 'revelation', 'inspiration' or 'authority'.

I turn now from testimony to thesis and, to make the transition, I offer another personal memory as a bridge. Possibly the most formative years of my life were the ten that we spent in Uganda, when I had to teach biblical studies and dogmatic theology in Luganda, a language devoid of genuine abstract terms. In neighbouring Kenya, Bishop Leonard Beecher was arguing persuasively that Swahili, with its vocabulary derived from Arabic and so, in many cases, from Hebrew or Greek roots, was best suited to become the theological lingua franca of East Africa, as Latin had been in Europe. For political reasons this would have been impossible in Uganda, and I am thankful that I was forced by the intractable concreteness of Luganda to ask myself time and time again what I really meant by a familiar theological term. This exercise opened my eyes to the fact that every concept we can have, including our idea of God, is derived from experience, our own or other people's, and then from subsequent reflection upon it. Consequently all revelation is mediated through things experienced on the physical plane, and true theology must inevitably be incarnational.

Consider how it is that we learned the meaning of any word you like to name. A baby fondles the family cat, not for the first time. That is the known *experience*. Close by, mother croons 'pussy cat'. That is the voice of *authority*, announcing what's what. Later, baby is being shown a new picture book. As the page turns, mother croons 'pussy cat' again. The picture looks very different from the familiar friend asleep on the sofa, but authority has spoken. From this interplay of authority and experience the child is learning a fundamental fact of language, namely that it depends upon basic likeness. All words are generalisations; they put experiences into categories. In fact, by some inborn skill which one would call reflection if the child were capable of discursive thought, the baby has already grasped this fact about language and embarrassed mother when out in the pram by greeting a passing male stranger as 'Dada'.

Within the next few years the child's concept of 'cat' is enriched by a wealth of *hearsay*. Do they have nine lives? Will a black one bring good luck? Is a lion really a cat? But in time the child's own maturer *reflection* can distinguish between old wives' tales, chance anecdotes and the authority of the school library. Authority may seem to have the last word; yet the first and originating word of all knowledge comes from experience, for even the authority of science has been derived from experience of what is there, subjected to reflection.

The same four sources contribute to our understanding of the word 'God', Far more than we care to admit, what we have in mind when we argue whether God exists or not, or when we take sides over the gender-language that should be applied to God, or when we answer a child's sudden questions about existence, is a mixed bag of popular hearsay, an unexamined stereotype. 'God is the supreme Being, distinct from all other beings. Because he is the one who made all other beings, he is all-powerful, able to do anything he chooses. He also knows everything that is going on. He is to be loved because he looks after us and wishes us well, but also feared because he punishes those who displease him. He is just, yet he doesn't appear to be; so when life is unfair we have to believe that he knows best. And when we die, if we have been good or if he forgives our sins, we will spend eternity with him and that will be blissful, though here and now it is hard to imagine.'

Maybe we should be grateful for the stereotype, flawed and misleading though it is. Without it the religious sense of humanity might have fragmented into an infinite hotchpotch of private opinions, the product of each individual's chance encounters with scraps of hearsay. The stereotype at least confers some kind of uniformity, though faulty; and this is because, in the background, giving it shape and continuity, there is a heritage of orthodox teaching. For all its inadequacies and distortions, the popular notion of God bears witness to the existence of an authoritative tradition, embodied in a creed, a code and a cult: what believers believe, how they behave, how they approach God.

All the great faiths of the world are defined, sustained and perpetuated by such a tradition, with official guardians to safeguard its continuity. That is what we mean by a religion. And most of the great faiths have a canon of scriptures in which the authority of the tradition resides with special weight. For Jews it is the Torah, with the rest of the Old Testament interpreted in the light of it, that speaks with the voice of a final authority. For Christians it is the New Testament, with the Old interpreted in the light of it. For Muslims the Qur'an is the definitive and final word of God to humanity. The Sikhs find the voice of authority in their Guru Granth Sahib, the Taoists in the humane precepts of the *Tao teh King*. There are differences in the degree to which the faithful of the various religions regard their sacred scriptures as God-given, but all alike attribute to them a unique authority.

So far, then, it would seem that a knowledge of what God is, is derived from garbled hearsay, corrected by some stable authority. Yet we have already seen that, in the human pursuit of knowledge, the voice of authority does not initiate the truth; it can only endorse and preserve and transmit the truth. The truth of anything can only be derived originally from experience of what is there, submitted to subsequent reflection. That is the point of the story of Newton's apple; and the later theory of relativity was not dreamed up by pure reason alone, but originated from the experience of observing deviations from the expected predictions of the speed with which light meets a moving object, such as a planet. Experience prompted new thought. So also we can 'know' that Mozart is one of the greatest composers, Shakespeare a supreme poet and dramatist, not because anyone decided to announce the fact in a book, but because, behind the books, lies the experience of all the people who have been moved and enlarged by that music or those words, and have pondered upon that experience, and asked why.

Of course, it may be objected that God is not a thing, an object that can be observed like an apple or a particle of energy, nor is God an immaterial quality to be experienced, like the impact of beauty. No one can 'see' God, that is, experience God direct, and live. As created beings, we can be made aware of God only as mediated through some created being. It may be the heavens that declare the glory of God, as we experience them with a particular wonderment; or it may be the silence created at the depth of our own hearts that announces God's presence. However it comes to us, there would be no revelation and no recognition unless God was making the approach. We would remain forever unaware of the possibility of God, we could have had no thought of him, if God had not been starting the rumour, calling attention to himself again and again. Nowhere has God left humanity without evidence of his presence and his nature.

The impact of beauty is not God, but it is a clue, a symbol, through which the reality of that which is absolutely other, wholly beyond, yet present within a created thing, is powerfully brought home to us. Experiences of the numinous, of confrontation with ultimate mystery, are very common and widespread. Moses' encounter at the burning bush (Exodus 3), Isaiah's vision in the temple (Isaiah 6), are paradigms of the *numinous* experience.

Equally common, and often combined with the numinous encounter, is a sudden revelation of the unity of all reality. Those who have experienced such glimpses will often say simply that they caught sight of 'the meaning of everything'. This is typical of all *mystical* experience.

A third general pattern of experience that brings home the presence and the nature of God is the impact of rescue. Every kind of personal or communal deliverance or reassurance is included in this category, and it is obvious that such *redemptive* experience is specially characteristic of the Bible stories.

There is another class of experience, which I would describe as the impact of personality. It covers the innumerable instances when a person, or occasionally a whole community, has been morally compelled to say of some other person, 'I saw God in that one.' These are rare encounters, and the one of whom it is said is often an obscure and humble man or woman. Like the other types of experience, this sort, when it happens, is incontrovertible and cannot be denied by the one who has known it.

Each of the great religions is a culturally-determined tradition of response and disobedience to these varied types of experience whereby the Lord God announces his presence and calls to humanity. Primal religion all over the world is mainly a response to numinous experiences: Hindu philosophy is a system of response to the mystical unitary vision; Judaism, Christianity and, to a lesser degree, Islam, are histories of response and disobedience to crucial corporate experiences of divine rescue; and everywhere, in the veneration of saints and gurus, but supremely in the apostles' experience of Jesus of Nazareth, we see response to the impact of human personality.

The Old and New Testaments, for all their bewildering detail, resemble a symphony in which all the variations, reversals and innovations are seen to be an exploration of four dominant and related themes. Four experiences are paramount – the Exodus, the Davidic Kingdom, the Babylonian Exile, and the event of Jesus Christ. All else is progressive pondering on the implications of these revelatory experiences. The centrality of all four of those experiences is evident when one thinks of the number of Christian hymns that draw on the imagery of redemption from slavery, desert wanderings and crossing Jordan, or the images of the Kingdom, the Holy City or the Temple of God, as well as those that sing directly of Jesus Christ. The sad exception is the Exile. Because of the triumph of Easter, Christians have generally failed to ponder on the experience of reversal and postponement, the note of 'Not yet', 'O Lord, how long, how long?', the alienation and endurance which feature in the New Testament as well as the Old. And this omission has, over the centuries, unnecessarily widened the rift of misunderstanding between ourselves and the Jewish faith.

Now, since it is revelation that the Bible is dealing with, what it presents to those who read it is the event *as experienced*, the impact of it, rather than the objective fact of the event in itself. From bits of evidence inside and outside the Bible, I suspect, as many have done, that the story of deliverance from Egypt, as it now stands in the book of Exodus, contains not only an overlay of successive accounts of one event, but details drawn from several distinct escape-stories experienced by various family groups of Hebrews over two or three hundred years. What is significant is that one such exodus, almost certainly associated with the leadership of Moses, was experienced as such a demonstration of divine rescue as to stand for ever as a definitive folk-memory, to which additional details from similar escapes might become attached, and from which generations of thinkers, law-givers and prophets drew momentous conclusions. I have no means of knowing precisely what happened objectively, nor does it matter. What I cannot doubt is that objective events did take place at some time, of such a kind as to convince the Hebrew clans who experienced them that none other than God had rescued them and adoped them as his own people for all time. I would want to say very much the same about the apostolic experience of the resurrection of Jesus.

Of course, the Bible does not confine itself to a narration of these four crucial experiences that are the core material of its revelation. It contains the continuous re-telling and re-living of the experiences, in hymns and ballads, rituals and festivals and sermons, whereby successive generations made them their story, their experience, and whereby we are still doing so. It contains lesser stories to demonstrate that the God of the Exodus continues to rescue, that the God of David still has a Kingdom and a City in view, that Jesus still heals and challenges and is Lord. So the Bible also presents the fruit of centuries of reflection upon the original experiences: the moral implications – 'Bear in mind that you were slaves in Egypt' (Deuteronomy 5–15 REB); 'Accept one another as Christ accepted us' (Romans 15.7); the theological implications, as grasped by the prophets – 'How can I give you up, Ephraim . . . for I am God and not a man?' (Hosea 11.8, 9); 'If we are faithless, he remains faithful' (2 Timothy 2–13)); the cosmological implications – creation itself has been a setting free, a letting go, and also an unconditional commitment on God's part like his commitment to Israel). The Bible also deals honestly with the problematic implications – 'I call for thy help, but thou dost not answer; I stand up to plead, but thou sittest aloof' (Job 30.20)) and shows the negative as well as the positive effects of the Exile experience of God's indefinite postponement of the promises.

The truth of these Scriptures is not prescriptive, spelled out once and for all like a creed, but evocative, eliciting assent as the original experiences did. So, in affirming the authority of our Scriptures we should remember that there are two levels of authority. There is an inherent authority that commands by being recognised, and a formal authority that commands by being conferred and empowered. One person may be acknowledged as an authority on Middle Eastern affairs. One person may be appointed to run the Middle East department at the Foreign Office. We may consider ourselves lucky if they are the same person! Jesus taught with an inherent authority which the common people were quick to recognise, unlike the scribes whose authority to teach had been officially conferred. The authority of the Bible is happily of both kinds. The Jewish Church, and later the Christian Church, conferred formal authority on these writings by including them, and not others, in the canon of Scripture. But they did so mainly because God's self-revelation, through the crucial experiences to which the Bible bears witness, grips and convinces those who read with its self-authenticating truth. The primary authority of Scripture lies in its power of speaking to our condition with the very voice of God.

That, you will tell me, is a very subjective criterion. I can only reply that conviction as to the truth about God must in the last resort be subjective, and it is the Bible that tells me so.

Since the heart of the biblical revelation lies in four crucial human experiences, we should pay more respect to the hazy and often arresting experiences of God reported by ordinary people, and stop smothering them with a hundred qualifications.

Since all the stories that make up such a large part of the Bible may be said to have God as their chief actor, yet all of them have a human being – such as Moses, David, Elijah, Paul – as their subject, it is time to recognise that God appears to have chosen, as a ground-rule of creation, never to act directly, but always through a created agent, and, for many purposes, always with a human partner. This applies especially to God's self-revelations, and so to the nature of Scripture.

God is consequently at risk as a condition inherent in the act of creation. We also are most likely to be close to God and in touch with the divine purpose when we too are without guarantees. The lessons of the Exile are more advanced than those of the Exodus. The experience of being safe in a storm-tossed boat because Christ is there at the stern must be followed by the experience of being in a storm-tossed boat with Christ out there on the waves, inviting us to join him in the greater security where he is, where God is, with five fathoms of uncertainty beneath his feet.

2

'THE BEGINNING OF THE GOSPEL IS NOTHING BUT THE WHOLE OLD TESTAMENT'

Alec Graham

This is the only title in this series which explicitly refers to the Old Testament. 'The beginning of the gospel is nothing but the whole of the Old Testament': that text or tag is a quotation, I believe, from Origen in the first half of the third century. I intend to use it as a peg on which to hang a number of points about the Old Testament and our use of it in the Church today.

First of all, what about the shape or *limits* of the Old Testament? Let us take up those words 'the whole Old Testament'. Nowadays this expression will convey different meanings to different groups of Christian people. For most Protestants 'the whole Old Testament' comprises those books which are to be found in the Hebrew Bible. Protestant Christians and Jews do not find these books in the same order in their respective Bibles, and this difference of order is itself evidence of the different ways in which the Bible is understood by Jews and by Christians. The Old Testament as used in the Roman Catholic Church will generally have the books which it uses in common with Jews and with Protestants in yet another order, and the Old Testament will be understood to include a wider range of writings which derive from the Greek Old Testament, the Septuagint. Yet the Council of Trent in the mid-sixteenth century decreed that certain of these books, namely the Prayer of Manasses and 1 and 2 Esdras, were not to be included in the Old Testament: in my copy of the Latin Bible they are printed as a sort of appendix, after the New Testament. As for the Bible used by the Orthodox Churches, there is, I suspect, some imprecision about the status of various books, and the list as generally received does not exactly coincide with the Old Testament and Apocrypha as received by Protestant Churches, or with the Old Testament and deuterocanonical works recognised by Roman Catholics. I mention some of these details to show that Origen's expression 'the whole Old Testament' has for us a certain imprecision about it. It sounds clear and definite enough, but on inspection we find that the term 'Old Testament' has some rough or blurred edges. In any case, it is clear that for the greater part of Christian history, that is, say, from the time of Origen until the time of the Reformation, the literary preparation for the gospel was generally understood to be the entire Greek Bible (the Septuagint), or the Latin Bible which had more or less the same contents; in other words it embraced both what most of us nowadays call the Old Testament and what we call the Apocrypha.

Now what about the *contents* of the Old Testament, however we may precisely define it? Are we expected to regard the entire contents of the Old Testament, the whole Old Testament in this sense, to be the beginning of the gospel? There is no doubt that the more we know about the world in which Jesus lived and about the intellectual and religious background to the world of the first few decades of the early Church, the better we shall be able to understand the gospel in its original setting. The more we know, for instance, about Judaism and other religious movements, and the more we know about the ways in which these movements interacted with Judaism, the better we shall be able to understand Jesus, St Paul and the spread of Christianity. Jesus was a Jew; Peter and Paul were Jews; most of the New Testament (perhaps even all of it) was written by Jews – Christian Jews indeed, but still Jews who had honoured the Jewish

Scriptures and had been instructed in them. The more familiar we are with Jewish literature of the period between the Testaments, with the ways in which the Scriptures themselves were understood and interpreted in Judaism at the beginning of the Christian era, and with other religious, philosophical and ethical writing in the Gentile world at that time, the better placed we shall be to appreciate the distinctive nature of the gospel. Most of all, if there is one thing needful for the understanding of the gospel, that one thing is the Old Testament. If we were allowed only one literary source to help us with our study of the gospel, it would be to the Old Testament that we would turn (even though, as we have seen, we may not be able to define precisely or to agree on what we understand by the Old Testament). Sir Edwyn Hoskyns used to tell his pupils at Cambridge that, when they studied their Greek New Testament they needed one other text, namely the Greek Old Testament. The reason for this is partly, as I have already stated, the fact that the New Testament authors had for the most part been nourished from infancy by the Jewish Scriptures, either in Hebrew or in Greek. These Scriptures deeply affected their piety, their outlook, their conduct; they lay at the heart of the religious tradition which had formed them and from which they came.

There is another, related, reason why the Jewish Scriptures, the whole Old Testament, are the beginning of the gospel: an apologetic reason. The earliest Christians had to justify their Christian faith; they had both to commend it and to defend it. Deepest of all their conviction was their belief that in Jesus, and subsequently in the Christian Church, was to be found the fulfilment of God's promises made of old to Israel – that is to say, made in the Old Testament – and reference to the Greek Old Testament would be more effective in the Gentile world than to the Scriptures in Hebrew. The Christian Church sprang from Judaism; it claimed to be the sole authentic heir to Judaism; it made exclusive claims about Jesus and justified them by appeal to the Old Testament; it used the Jewish Scriptures and maintained that it alone understood their true and proper meaning.

Very boldly, and from the outset, the earliest Christians, even before there was any specifically, explicitly, Christian literature, said that the Old Testament was their book; they alone knew what it meant. Before there were any Christian Scriptures to guide them, these earliest Christians looked to the Old Testament as their work of reference and written authority; they had no other, and they believed that no one else understood it properly. So, when defending the Christian gospel or when trying to convince others of the truth of the Christian gospel, it was from the Old Testament that they drew their support and their ammunition.

The Old Testament later provided the general framework of reference and also points of detail in the argument. Sometimes the argument may have seemed quite a *tour de force*, but it was an argument and an approach capable of being appreciated both by Jews and also by Gentile sympathisers who were familiar with the Jewish Scriptures. As Jesus' own understanding of the Jewish law was in some respects radically different from the way in which it was understood by Jewish orthodoxy in his day, and as Jesus himself fell foul of the Jewish religious leaders of his time, the argument from the Old Testament (and there was no other authority to which to appeal) had to be pressed home very hard and very ingeniously. Moreover, it was pressed home in ways which would have had some chance of carrying conviction in his day and in the first decades of the young Church. Thus not only was the Old Testament the beginning of the gospel; we shall also be helped to understand the beginning of the gospel if we know something about the methods of exegesis, the techniques of understanding and application, employed with regard to the Old Testament at the turn of the Christian era.

But is it indeed the whole Old Testament which is the beginning of the gospel, as is maintained in our text from Origen? Surely we could make a case that it is only part or, more exactly, parts of the Old Testament to which we have to turn and which are so employed. Some of us were brought up a couple of generations ago on the thesis that the New Testament writers drew principally on certain particular passages of the Old Testament and that these passages were, as a consequence, to be regarded as of especial importance in the formation of the Gospels and of the New Testament as a whole. In a familiar form this thesis maintained that it was not merely the particular verse or verses quoted which were being used to support Christian claims or were being given a Christian interpretation; rather, the entire passage or the total context was being understood to speak of Christ.[1] Indeed it is undeniable that certain passages seem frequently to have been used as quarries for Christian preaching and apologetics, for instance parts of Hosea and Zechariah, of Joel and Daniel; sections of the prophecy of Isaiah, and not just those which bear upon the Servant; certain Psalms, too, have been particularly influential. But that is far from 'the whole Old Testament'. Can Origen's reference to 'the whole Old Testament' be sustained in this connection? The answer surely is yes, and it is yes in three quite distinct respects.

1. It is no exaggeration to say that there is no chapter of the Gospels or of the entire New Testament which does not contain a quotation from, or an allusion to, or an echo of the Old Testament. Some editions of the Greek New Testament italicise or otherwise draw attention to the clearest quotations from the Old Testament. Some of the modern English translations of the New Testament draw to the reader's attention in footnotes the principal passages of the Old Testament on which a New Testament author has drawn. But in using that expression 'on which a New Testament author has drawn', are we asserting more than the evidence requires? Surely in some passages, indeed in very many passages, the quotation or allusion is so clear that we have to suppose that the author intended us to look back to a passage from the Old Testament, to bear it in mind, to use it in our understanding of his own work. I admit that here we are on slippery ground: it is important not to be dogmatic about the intentions of authors, particularly of authors whose conventions and outlook are often so different from those of our day.

Nevertheless, explicit quotations, or some other clear reference to a passage, incident or personage in the Old Testament, is surely warrant enough for us to suppose that our author made the quotation as a beacon or pointer so that he who runs may read (as Habakkuk put it).

Beside explicit quotation and clear reference there are countless other instances in which we hear, or think we hear, echoes, allusions, overtones, resonances which take our minds to persons or incidents or passages or themes from the Old Testament. No one can tell how much of this is the fruit of the conscious intention of the New Testament author. Some of it may well be; some of it may be the natural and instinctive way whereby a person brought up in a particular religious or literary tradition will unconsciously or spontaneously express himself in words and images which have become part of his very being, so long has he lived them or been nourished by them. In English literature, for instance, the more widely read a person is, the more echoes and overtones of earlier authors he will detect in whatever he is reading, and the better able he will be to appreciate and wonder at the richness of the tapestry and the complexity of the texture with which he is engaged. Further, though no one should dogmatise about the mysterious process of literary creation (or indeed of any type of artistic creation), it cannot be denied that, in a work like the book of Revelation, images, ideas, patterns, words and phrases from the Old Testament, particularly the books of Ezekiel, Daniel and Zechariah, have been taken up and mysteriously transformed in the creative mind and imagination of one who was an early Christian visionary, poet and prophet.

So, while it is often impossible to be precise about the allusions or references which a New Testament author intended to make, or about the conclusions (if any) which he intended us to draw from his use of a reference from or of an allusion to the Old Testament, nevertheless the New is simply saturated with material from the Old Testament. The more familiar we are with the Old Testament in its broadest sense, the more of these overtones and undertones we shall be able to detect. All of that will constitute, on our part, a layer of understanding or appreciation for which our reading of the New Testament will be all the richer, more rewarding, and more likely to lead to the discovery of unsuspected depths. It is the whole Old Testament of which we find echoes in the New; there is scarcely a book of the Old Testament which is not drawn upon in this way. As we read the New Testament, we shall be wise to keep our eyes on the text and our ears open to the passages from the Old Testament which are suggested to us by our reading.

2. It is the whole Old Testament on which we draw as we begin to study the gospel, not just in that there is quotation from, or reference to, or echo of, pretty well every part of the Old Testament; also in the sense that the great themes which the New Testament writers treat have their roots and their early history in the Old Testament. The New Testament writers share many of the principal presuppositions of the Old Testament, and there are certain grand themes and convictions which figure prominently in the entire Bible: themes about God and about mankind; the world and mankind's place within it; ethical demand and righteous behaviour; community and covenant; election and purpose; God's rule and sovereignty on earth and in heaven, in time and for eternity; a beginning and an end. These are some of the controlling themes of the entire Bible; they underlie every part of the Old Testament, even those where they may not receive explicit mention. They are all picked up, enlarged and to a degree transformed in various ways by the New Testament writers. Despite a variety of viewpoints to be found within both the Old Testament and the New, there are also common fundamental convictions. If we start with the New Testament, we shall be driven back to the Old in order to pick up the framework of thought and to learn the underlying presuppositions. In the days when I was responsible for the studies of undergraduates, they were normally introduced first to the Old Testament, then to the New. One year, as an experiment,

we followed the reverse order, and the undergraduates complained that without some knowledge of the Old Testament, they could not make sense of what they found in the New. Christ and Kingdom, Spirit, Word and Wisdom, sacrifice and covenant, law and grace – all of these great themes of the Christian dispensation, cannot be understood without some knowledge of the great sweep of the Old Testament in which they are treated in a variety of ways. Also, and of equal importance, there are those presuppositions of the Old Testament writers which are often tacitly assumed even in those passages where they do not come to the surface. In this sense 'the beginning of the gospel' is nothing but the whole Old Testament, every part of it important for illuminating the Christian revelation, for, put at its simplest, the God and Father of Our Lord Jesus Christ is believed to be none other than the God of Abraham, Isaac and Jacob.

3. There is a third reason why it is the whole Old Testament with which we have to do: simply, that the entire Old Testament (ill-defined, though it may be at its edges) has been given to us. The entire Bible is like some great erratic boulder against which the student of literature and of history and of religion strikes his foot; that is equally true of the Old Testament considered separately and in its own right. It is a most remarkable collection of texts; its process of compilation must have taken the greater part of one thousand years; it contains an astonishing variety of material: saga and history, legal codes and prophetic oracles, wise sayings and predictions about the coming end, hymns and poems, some meditative, some triumphant, some questioning, some accepting. Those are the principal broad categories, and within each category much of the material has been adapted and shaped to meet the successive needs of the people of Israel. There are little books with their own particular atmosphere, one (Esther) redolent of the Arabian Nights, another (the Song of Songs) apparently a collection of love lyrics. Hidden away in the mass of this material, there are fragments on

which we may stumble and which originally may have served, surely, as a night watchman's cry (Isaiah 21.11f) or as a prostitute's invitation (Isaiah 23.15f) or as a rubric to a liturgy. I mention some of these details in order to convey some impression of the astonishing range of the literary contents of the Old Testament, both in their span of time and in the variety of their material. This variegated mass of material has been collected, treasured, translated and handed on down the centuries. To the believing Christian, as to the believing Jew, it is God's gift, all of it, and it is not for us to pick and choose. The Jew, it is true, will regard the first five books of the Bible as pre-eminently authoritative. Sometimes the Christian may have regarded the predictive work of the prophets as especially significant. But properly the entire Old Testament is to be regarded as God's gift to us for us to receive and reverence and use.

'Nothing human is indifferent to me' might well have been a motto for the authors of the books of the Old Testament, for all their thinking and activity was undertaken within a framework of belief in the creator God, who had placed human beings in his world, to reverence it, to obey him, and to order their lives as individuals and in society in ways consonant with his providential ordering of the universe. By contrast the New Testament is very much the product of a small, restless, alien body within the wider Graeco-Roman world: many of its preoccupations centre round the proper ordering of the interior life of the believing community. On the other hand, the Old Testament writers often feel able to express their own instinctive, natural, unredeemed hopes and fears, hates and ambitions: their despair or longing or their hatred and revenge help us to see how all this can be transcended in Christ. The rough humanity of the Old Testament needs to be received in its fullness: the entire Old Testament is 'the beginning of the gospel'. For the Christian it provides the background and the context for understanding the Christian gospel: more still, it reveals the wide range of human needs which the Christian believes Christ came to meet; even more it embraces the entire creation (and humanity within it) which Christ came, we believe, to restore and bring to fulfilment.

Further, unlike many of the authors of the New Testament who tend to concentrate more on the internal affairs of the young Church, the Old Testament writers are often concerned about the right ordering of society as a whole. In different centuries Christian people have returned to their inheritance in the Old Testament and concentrated on different parts of it, deriving from it material which they believe speaks to their age and their need. In the time of the Tudors and early Stuarts, the Old Testament provided the ideal of the godly prince and legitimated the divine right of kings. Intermittently throughout Christian history the Old Testament prophets' denunciation of injustice has made itself heard, together with its sharp reminders to the influential and powerful. More recently the story of the Exodus has served as the inspiration of an entire school of theology (liberation theology), and today reference is often made to the books of the law with their detailed provision for the proper way to run society – with regard to the Sabbath, to debt, to the need to make provision for the disadvantaged. It is not surprising that this vast literary enterprise, which owes its present shape to such a variety of personal and social circumstances, should prove so endlessly creative: different strands or different parts make themselves felt, appeal to and speak to different circumstances. In this sense too it is the entire Old Testament which proves to be 'the beginning of the gospel', both of its understanding and of its application. It is important to resist the recurrent temptation to cut it down to size by claiming that only parts of it are relevant, or that there are certain correct answers to the problems which it raises, or certain approved methods of interpretation which alone are acceptable nowadays. On one level it is certainly great literature, on another it is believed to be the Word of God: in neither respect can there be clear, neat, safe, correct answers, and in both respects it has its own life and its own creative power.

That said, most of us have received the Old Testament within the tradition of the Christian Church, and the Church has come to have a common mind about some of the ways in which Christian people appropriately use and understand the Old Testament. For instance, we believe that it finds its fulfilment in Christ, and we read it refined and refracted through Christian lenses. Within those general principles, there are some detailed matters with regard to the understanding of the Old Testament about which the Christian Church is quite clear. For instance, long ago the Christian Church came to realise that certain ways of interpreting Proverbs 8 and its bearing on the person of Christ were consistent with Christian belief, and others not. More recently, there has emerged a consensus among Christian people that the proper way to understand relationships between the races is not to be governed by an exegesis of the significance of Shem, Ham and Japheth, let alone by setting forward a policy based on Nehemiah 13.

So there are certain respects in which Christian people have come to a common mind about the understanding of the Old Testament; equally, we are invited to sit down under the Old Testament, all of it, to perceive the appropriate ways to use it nowadays and to receive its message for us and for our time. We can reflect on a great sentence from Coleridge (the exact words of which, alas, I have not been able to trace) who wrote of God's marching up and down the pages of Scripture, bringing it to life magisterially where he will. Indeed he does, and we are to wait until he does so. In the meanwhile the Old Testament, indeed all the Scriptures, are God's gift to us. There is inevitably a good deal of roughage, but it is only as we chew at the entire fare provided for us that we derive the nourishment which it brings.

This conviction about the givenness of Scripture, in our case of the Old Testament, lies behind a way of understanding the biblical material which goes by the name of canonical criticism and is associated with the writing of Brevard Childs.[2] It takes as its starting point the canon of Scripture, whole, unvarnished and untarnished, as it has been received by us. We have already noted that the canon of the Old Testament proves to be a more elusive, shifting phenomenon than is often supposed, and that is a major difficulty so far as this approach is concerned. But this school of canonical critics takes the entire text seriously, and they take seriously the entire text of each book in its final form as received by us. In taking the whole text as their starting point, they underline for us that the entire Scripture is, as it were, a *datum*, a thing given: it is not for us to pay attention only to the fashionable bits or to the popular bits: it is the entire text which is on offer, and it is on offer in the form in which it is presented to us in our Bibles. This strikes an echoing chord in my own experience: I had never understood why, in studying the book of Job, we were supposed (according to the critical orthodoxy of the time) not to pay attention to the speeches of Elihu: it always seemed to me that they were integral to the structure of the book as we had received it. How did people know, I wondered, that they were added almost as an afterthought; even if they were an afterthought, they must have originated in the mind of some author, and some editor must have seen fit to include them in the book; so why were we not supposed to give them serious consideration when we were trying to appreciate the message of the book as a whole? It would be equally foolish to refuse to pay attention to the Gothic alterations or to the Baroque decoration of a basically Romanesque cathedral, unless, of course, one had a dogmatic presupposition that only the primitive form was worthy of attention. Or, to take a rather different example from the study of the Psalms: in recent times scholarly study of the psalms has tended to concentrate on the background of each psalm and on their early history and meaning. However, the book of Psalms has come to us as a whole, and I never understood why we were not allowed to consider the book as a whole, nor to attend to the great variety of ways in which the psalms had been understood during their history. Why, I wondered, was the original setting and meaning (themselves often no more than conjectural) thought to be definitive for all time? Canonical criticism has come in for some pretty devastating censure, and we cannot here rehearse all the arguments about it, but it does remind us that a holy God stands over against us and has presented us with this given thing, holy Scripture old and new; further, it maintains and reminds us that the biblical text as a whole needs to be interpreted in relation to a community of faith and practice in regard to which it has divine authority.

It will be obvious that canonical criticism stands in marked contrast to and reaction against certain consequences of the way in which the movement of biblical criticism has for the most part treated Scripture. Perhaps it would be true to say that the critical movement paid full justice to the entire humanness of the Scriptures and of their authors; that it tended to discern and isolate the original words or events around which a text had been built or had evolved; that it resulted in a certain atomising of the biblical message; that on occasions it fell into the fallacy of supposing that one could even be certain about the original intention of the original author, or of supposing that the original shape was necessarily purer than all others. In common with quite a number of modern literary approaches to biblical study, canonical criticism takes Scripture as a whole: these holistic approaches (as the modern jargon calls them) are often basically un-historical or even anti-historical; some of them are frankly uninterested in the content of Scripture, but they have this in common: they take the entire literary unit – in our case the Old Testament (though, as we have seen, with rough edges), and they get to work on the text before them, following up clues and patterns, themes and symbols to be found within the text itself.

We pass on to two unfashionable, unpopular uses of Scripture, which also treat the biblical text as a whole and in the form given to us. These both deserve to be rehabilitated.

1. The treatment of biblical theology, and within it of Old Testament theology, needs to be revived. The movement of biblical theology, which I suppose reached its peak in the 1950s and early 1960s came as a great relief to many students of the

Scriptures and a great source of enrichment to many preachers and believers. It concentrated on the content of the biblical books: it took seriously the conviction that the Bible is the Church's book from which it teaches, and not only the book of the scholars for whom it is a field of research. It sprang from an expectation that within the Bible (or, for that matter, within each Testament) we should expect to find some coherence of viewpoint in general and on specific theological topics.

No doubt the movement had weaknesses. For instance, it may have so emphasised the unity of the Bible or of each Testament that it failed to do justice to the variety of viewpoints to be found within it, each of which is characteristic of a particular author or school or era. Related to this point is another: namely, that the movement of biblical theology sometimes stated its conclusions too aggressively or assertively, as if there were but one answer to any question or one line on any subject: we recall the very titles of some of those formative books, for instance *The Biblical Doctrine of Election*; *The Biblical Doctrine of Work* – as if there were but one doctrine on each subject and the author had mastered it. The facts may well be more subtle and complex than these titles may imply: yet we should suppose that beneath this variety of approach and viewpoint, within even the Old Testament one should be able to discern underlying convictions common to all the authors of the Old Testament works. Further, the identification of different approaches to particular problems in different times and circumstances can help us to discover the richness and variety of the biblical material. Unlike the biblical theologians of thirty or forty years ago we shall need to draw on the whole Old Testament; some tended to concentrate on certain themes and on certain books and to neglect or underplay the Wisdom literature and the emerging apocalyptic movement. Also they tended to be strong on attention to the text, but weak on context, and it is the context which will help to explain for us the variety of viewpoint.

So the first of these two unfashionable uses of Scripture which are in need of revival is the study of biblical theology. For this the entire Old Testament must be field of study; only thus shall we be able to appreciate the richness and the diversity and the distinctiveness of its teaching and message.

2. Now for the other unfashionable use of the whole Old Testament: the exploration of its mystical senses. We might call them generically the mystical, or the spiritual, or the figurative, and within them we might distinguish the allegorical, the typological and the devotional. They are all despised nowadays: the allegorical because of its indifference to history; the typological because of its forced treatment of texts and because of its disregard for context; the devotional because it smacks of pietism and thus is understood to interfere with clarity of thought. Yet taken together these mystical, spiritual, figurative understandings have been the ways in which the Church has understood Scripture most consistently through the centuries. If we look to the past for guidance on how to use Scripture, we shall find that over the centuries these figurative or mystical senses have occupied centre stage. The Church would probably not have been able to retain and use the Old Testament if it had not been for the convenient availability of this use of the sacred text. All those indecent, unbecoming, obscure, textually corrupt, apparently contradictory passages could be used, understood and treated as the vehicle to something better, either deeper or higher. Allegory is there all right in the Old Testament; Jotham's fable (Judges 9.7ff) is the obvious example. St Paul himself tells us in one passage that he is treating what we call the Old Testament allegorically (Galatians 4.24). The allegorical use of Scripture takes the given text with full seriousness and digs into it. No doubt it is unhistorical, but not everything in Scripture is of historical interest or amenable to historical treatment. The law-codes are a case in point; allegory may be a useful homilectic device for the understanding of this type of material.

In any case, allegory shades off into typology, and both into the devotional. Let us glance at the typological approach. This, too, operates from and within the given text of Scripture; it assumes that the actions of God have a measure of unity, consistency and inner coherence. We find it employed even within the Old Testament itself. Was not reference made to the crossing of the river Jordan, and later to the return from exile, in terms which take the reader's mind to the crossing of the Red Sea? Do not the first creation narrative and the story of Noah's ark bear upon the same theme? The various passages are variants upon a common theme and illuminate one another. More still, typology is a marvellously useful tool for doing justice to the unity which Christians believe exists between the Old Testament and the New.

These two uses of the text of the Old Testament, the allegorical and the typological, merge into the devotional. We may find them strange and arbitrary, and indeed they can be used in ways that are either merely ingenious or downright capricious. Yet these uses of the Old Testament are close to the way in which Jesus himself may have used it; certainly close to the ways in which it was understood in his time and for the greater part of the history of the Church. These uses have inspired so much in painting and sculpture, in theological exegesis and devotional writing, in hymnody and liturgy. We see this inspiration very clearly in some of the great hymns which have come down to us from the middle ages; we see it also in hymns with quite different provenance, for instance in 'Guide me, O thou great Redeemer' from the Welsh evangelical revival: the couplet 'When I tread the verge of Jordan, bid my anxious fears subside; Death of death, and hell's destruction, land me safe on Canaan's side' is a veritable mosaic of instances of figurative, allusive, typological, transferred uses of Scripture, both Old and New.

This use of Scripture has certainly nourished the Church in other respects: we find it in some of the collects in The Book of Common Prayer. The Solemnization of Matrimony provides several examples of this use of material from the Old Testament with its reference to Adam and Eve, Abraham and Sarah, Isaac and Rebecca; the passage which refers to 'the spiritual marriage and unity betwixt Christ and His Church' takes the mind not only to the fifth chapter of the Epistle to the Ephesians, but also to the chapter headings to the Song of Solomon in the Authorised Version. We find another excellent example in the first prayer at the Publick Baptism of Infants, which refers to the narrative about Noah and to the Exodus as 'figuring' holy baptism. Some of this rich material, partly typological, partly devotional, some even allegorical, has survived in The Alternative Service Book, though in an attenuated and etiolated form. It has survived there because it is so deeply rooted in the history of Christian doctrine and liturgy; it has been deeply rooted there from the time of the New Testament onwards, and it took deep root then because the whole Old Testament and no less than the whole Old Testament was understood to be 'the beginning of the gospel'.

We have stated a case for the revival of two uses of Scripture. One, the movement of biblical theology, did indeed take seriously the critical study of Scripture, but it was (as we have seen) more interested in content. The other, the pursuit of the mystical senses of Scripture, frankly has no time for critical study of the Scripture such as has been pursued in scholarly circles for well over a century. These two unfashionable uses have this in common: they treat Scripture as the Church's book given to us to receive, to believe, to come to terms with and to hand on. There is a danger here, and we need to be on our guard. The danger is that the Bible may be understood as if it revolves simply in its own closed world, and that, as we study it and learn from it, we may become locked into that same sealed world. We have noted that on occasions biblical theology gave the impression of presenting the world with *the* biblical answer to its problems, almost of dictating *the* Christian solution to the world's difficulties on certain matters. It did, as we have seen, pay insufficient attention to the variety of viewpoints and of contexts characteristic of the biblical authors; also, there was insufficient engagement with the world and insufficient theological engagement with God's activity and presence in the world. We find a similar weakness with regard to the mystical, spiritual use of Scripture; they can easily lead the believer, the worshipper and the prayer to be locked into a private world of mystic correspondences and of coded messages, a world which bears little obvious relation to the world outside and would be scarcely comprehensible outside.

This brings me to the point: the recovery of these two ways of understanding Scripture, in our case the Old Testament, does not relieve us of the necessity to continue the critical study of the Bible; indeed, critical study assumes even greater importance. After all, the critical study of Scripture, of authorship, of dating, of the process of literary formation, of historical background, is bound to affect any conclusions reached by biblical theologians or by theologians of the Old Testament. At least a provisional judgement will have to be made, on the basis of the best evidence available, about the historical and critical questions which are raised by the very text of the Old Testament. Some conclusion, however tentative, will have to be reached about the Exodus: whether it happened, what happened and when; for (to put it mildly) if we conclude that nothing happened, that conclusion is bound to affect our understanding of wide areas of Israel's beliefs and practices. Or, to take another obvious example, our understanding of certain biblical books is bound to be affected by our answers, however provisional and tentative, to questions about the circumstances of their origin. For instance: Was the book of Daniel written in the second century BC or not? Is the entire book of the prophet Isaiah to be understood as deriving from the time of Isaiah of Jerusalem? How do we explain the chronological difficulties apparent on the surface of the books of Ezra and Nehemiah? Our answers to questions such as these will affect our understanding of the Bible's content and message.

The Scriptures are not timeless in their origins: we shall appreciate their message as we come to appreciate the context of their production. Equally, our devotional use of Scripture, as well as our theological use, will be the richer for our appreciation of context – literary, historical, sociological, religious. Experience tells that when Scripture is wrestled with, shaken and tested, probed and investigated, then it yields its secret. Sometimes it is maintained that scholarly study of Scripture and serious engagement with it according to our lights, is nothing other than a waste of time for the believer, since scholarly conclusions are, so it is said, but shifting sands. Not infrequently this contention conceals a disinclination for hard study or for the questioning of presuppositions; in other words it may conceal idleness or timidity. Rather, by engaging with the critical and historical study of Scripture, we shall be enabled to appreciate better the text, the context and the contents; any conclusions will be provisional, and they may be contested or controversial, but we have a duty to grapple with the problems raised by the given material. If this is true of any one book of the Old Testament, it must be true of 'the whole Old Testament', and indeed of the entire Bible. We use our critical faculties on the Bible in order that we may the better discern its message to us and its judgement on us.

The time has come to conclude. Our subject has been the Old Testament – the entire Old Testament. Despite imprecision about the exact extent of the Old Testament we have seen how the Christian Church has claimed it for itself and drawn on it in its entirety. We have advocated a revival of two old-fashioned ways of drawing on and understanding the entire text of the Old Testament. These ways have taken us to an area touched on by others in this series, to liturgy and to prayer, to worship, public and private. It is appropriate that we have touched on this area, for we properly maintain that within the worshipping life and membership of the Church the message of Scripture stands the best chance of being understood, since it was handed on and written from faith to faith. That said, there are plenty of ways of understanding and using Scripture: some may be bizarre; some conclusions have been discouraged or even prohibited by the Church. But generally the field is open; there are many ways of understanding Scripture – historical, traditio-historical, critical, lexical, text-critical, sociological, political, literary, figurative, devotional, doctrinal, and so on. Some of these uses sit uneasily beside one another, but why not recognise them all as legitimate? The more varied our approach to, and our use of, Scripture, the more likely we are to appreciate its mystery and its richness, and the more likely it is to divulge its secret to us. It is the entire body of Scripture which has been given to us for us to investigate with our critical faculties, to discern its doctrine with our believing minds and to feed on in devotion. The entire body of Scripture is both Word of God and word of man; it is with the whole Old Testament that we have to do. For, as we have seen, the Old Testament is in so many respects nothing less than 'the beginning of the gospel'.

3

WHO IS REALLY IN CHARGE –
BIBLE OR CHURCH?

Peter Selby

Before all else, I have had to decide where it is I stand as I tackle the question of how I regard and use the Bible, and whether it is the Church or the Bible that is in charge. Some time ago the question, 'Where do you stand?' was focused very sharply for me as I looked out over the crowds of miners and their supporters waiting on Newcastle Central station for the charter train they had booked to go to London. And if a large gathering of workpeople met to protest on behalf of their jobs and our future raised that question in my mind, so of course do a hundred and one other places where we find ourselves standing. Which are the governing experiences that come into your heart and mind as you hold the Scriptures in your hand or turn over their pages?

This question presses upon us inescapably because we all know how varied have been the stances towards the Bible taken up in the centuries since it took its present shape. We know that those who have wanted to control others have had recourse to the Bible to assist them; we know that those who have sought God's aid and succour in their revolt against the tyranny of others have had resort to the Bible. We know that those who have sought a word of judgement, whether against others or against themselves, on conduct of which they disapproved, have found it easily in the Bible, while those who have sought words of forgiveness or release have found them there too.

We cannot forget that those who sought racial justice in South Africa found strong and empowering support in the Scriptures, while against them those who believed in the separation of the races declared that their firm convictions could be equally well buttressed by biblical quotation. General Synod members on either side of the debate about the ordination of women to the priesthood have based their arguments on Scripture. We may like to think that we all come to the Scriptures fresh, with minds open to whichever way the text may lead us, or, if we are academic researchers, that we are blessed with intellectual objectivity; but we cannot erase from our minds the knowledge we have of the biases that have been brought towards biblical interpretation throughout Christian history. We are therefore unlikely to be able to deceive ourselves for long into supposing that we are the first generation of those who approach the Bible with cool disinterest.

The overall theme of this series is, 'how *I* regard and use the Bible'; that is, I have been asked to be personal. I am to provide some kind of a window into the place of the Bible in my faith and, if I dare, my life. I have also been asked to give my contribution as one of a series of eight bishops; that means that I ought to have something to say about how my life as a bishop is affected by the Bible, either because the fact of being a bishop has itself changed my view about the Bible or at least because as a bishop I ought to have thought this matter through and attained some clarity about it.

So I shall seek to be personal and at the same time to share some of the perceptions that have come my way as a bishop. But my personal and episcopal reflections are about something objective around which we all gather: the Bible, the sacred text of the Christian community. Compared with that text, my perceptions as a bishop, let alone my personal insights and experience are, to use a word to which I shall have later to return, very much 'subtext'.

We are concerned therefore with text and with subtext. But we have first to take note of some crucial issues which arise from our *context*. What I have to say in this respect is perhaps blind-ingly evident, but it is important.

To state the obvious; I am a man who is white, middle-class and English. I am bound, therefore, to present the Bible in certain ways, some of which are in my conscious awareness, and some of which are not. Furthermore, this whole series is being given by eight bishops who are all Anglicans and have all exercised, or now exercise, the functions of a bishop in England. If our concern is to learn how particular persons regard and use the Bible, we need to be aware of the limited national and social background from which our sample is chosen and from which, with very few exceptions, all Church of England bishops are chosen.

And if our concern is with how bishops in particular view the Bible, we need to be aware, first, that by no means all bishops who work in England are Anglican: there are Roman Catholic and Pentecostal and Orthodox bishops, as well as many others in positions of leadership who exercise an episcopal office even if without the title. We need to be aware, secondly, that only a minority of Anglican bishops work in England: there are Anglican bishops throughout the world; they are of diverse ethnic backgrounds and indeed, if I may mention a cloud no larger than a person's hand, there are women among them. (You will recall that the cloud described in that way was the first sign of the end of a devastating drought.)

So my text, like the text of Scripture, has a context; I am the person I am, and not another. Further, this contribution, and the whole series, has a context in another sense: the subject did not, I imagine, come out of the air. It is a fact that almost all the major debates recently or currently going on in the Church of England appear to turn in the end on the fundamental position taken by the various 'sides' on the authority of the Bible and its interpretation. I say 'appear to' because, as I have written elsewhere,[1] I do not accept a Gilbertian description of the Church of England as one in which

> Every boy and every girl
> That's born into the world alive
> Is either a little Liberal
> Or else a little Conservative.

I believe that more basic issues are at stake; nevertheless those basic issues are reflected in attitudes to the Bible, and part of our context is that the issue of how the Bible is to be regarded is a very current one.

That means, for instance, that we are likely to hear what any representative figures in the Church of England say about the Bible as a more or less coded way of also telling us what they think about other things: at the moment we are likely to 'decode' what they say as telling us what they think about the ordination of women; in 1987 maybe we should have been more likely to assume they were telling us what they thought about homosexuality; in 1984 we should have deduced what they were likely to be thinking about the supposed views of the Bishop of Durham; and so on.

So our concern has to be with our context and not just our text: Who are we who are examining this question, and how does this question come to be examined by us at this particular time? If you are inclined to think this is just preamble, let me put this to you: suppose for example you were one of that huge crowd of miners and supporters I mentioned, gathered on Newcastle station. And suppose that there and then someone – perhaps even I myself dressed as a bishop – had stood on a box and started to talk about the Bible. How readily do you think people would have listened? And what do you think would have been their immediate suspicion about the speaker and what they were going to suggest the Bible's message would be? Or ask yourself what this series would have been like if a group of Irish bishops were giving their views on the Bible: would we not be watching all the time to know what they really thought about the relation of the two communities in Northern Ireland? Or imagine the contribution that would be brought by eight Pentecostal bishops, caring for the large number of predominantly African Christians living in our cities.

Surely we all know that what they would have to say would be different from what we are saying, and that the difference would not come from the fact that they were simply different individuals speaking or listening, but from the different contexts that had formed their minds or were occupying their attention. So the context affects profoundly, perhaps more profoundly when we are not aware of its effect, what is said and what is heard.

Furthermore, there is a particular piece of context that we cannot ignore in relation to our subject in this series. We are concerned with the Bible, the sacred text of the Christian community. And our context is now a world which has for centuries had many sacred texts, including some far older than anything in our Bible. The knowledge of that huge variety of sacred texts is now widely dispersed, so that any discussion of any sacred text has to take that aspect of our context seriously. The texts are not new; but the consciousness of them is. Nobody who makes the claim that the Christian Scriptures contain the message of salvation for the whole world can avoid encountering the perception in our time that such a claim has direct implications for the status of other sacred texts.

So our concern with the subtext of our own lives and the text of the Bible takes us straight into facing the context in which we are operating: our personal context, our context within the Church at large, with its particular concerns and debates, and our context as citizens of a world in which human consciousness is in a process of change that is both profound and swift.

Immediately I say this I have to go on to say that these aspects of being concerned about a text – the aspects of context and subtext – are very close to the preoccupations of all those engaged in biblical scholarship. We have left behind the era when we could be content that to subject a text to criticism could simply mean looking at the ancient biblical manuscripts so as to seek to determine which is the correct reading of a particular word or sentence. In common with those who study literature of all kinds, biblical scholars are concerned with 'text', with the whole range of factors which have led to our having before us the text we have, and indeed with all the layers of oral and written tradition that have gone into its making.

Part of our text, then, is that we live, unavoidably, as the heirs of several centuries of the critical study of Scripture. As in so many aspects of life, there is a debate going on all the time between those who are classed as 'conservative' and those who are classed as 'progressive' or 'liberal'. But whatever may be the disagreements between them are as nothing compared with the gulf that separates all of us from our forebears who had not had the experience of using the methods of historical, literary and other forms of criticism on the biblical text.

So when I raise the question, 'Who is really in charge – Bible or Church?' I have to be clear that I cannot be asking that question as it has been raised in the long centuries in which that issue has been debated. The uncompromising assertion that it is the Bible that has primary authority was a mainspring of the Reformation, and Article 6 of the Thirty-Nine Articles states, over against the perceived claims of the Roman Catholic Church the conviction that 'whatsoever is not read therein or may be proved thereby is not to be required of any man, that it should be believed as an article of the Faith, or be thought requisite or necessary for salvation.' Yet our concern has to be, not with the problem of a church authority requiring people to believe what cannot be proved out of the Bible, but rather with a situation where the authority for any interpretation has been cast into doubt through generations of biblical criticism and through features of our context which none of us can escape. Where may we suppose that authority is to be found – or is there none left?

It is these two themes of context and authority that are my main concern. To put in two sentences what I wish to say: first, I regard the Bible as speaking to human beings *in their context*, and in the process it redefines what their real context is; and secondly, to the question, 'Who is really in charge – Bible or Church?' the Bible responds by proposing a quite different understanding of what it is to be 'in charge', that is, of the nature of authority.

To begin with the matter of authority, I look back over the years since theology became a consuming interest of mine, and see as a constant feature a dialogue with Evangelical Christian friends, a dialogue which was, I am glad to say, strengthened while I was working as a bishop. Early on in my student days, an evangelical friend encouraged me to read James Packer's *Fundamentalism and the Word of God*.[2] I think the encouragement was accompanied by much prayer that I might be converted away from my rather too strong attachment to the ideas contained in John Robinson's *Honest to God*! Packer's argument seemed to me at the time to have an attractive simplicity about it: we all accept some authority as final, and in the case of Christian faith it will either be the Bible or the Church or our human reason; there are overwhelming arguments (which Packer details) against either the Church or human reason being final arbiter in matters of faith, and so the Bible must have that role.

Despite Packer's book, the encouragement and the prayer, however, I came to find the attractiveness of that simple argument very superficial. The claim that we all have to have some final authority in matters of faith prompts the same reaction as the claim by those who want to keep 'obey' in the marriage service on the grounds that all families 'have to have' someone who takes the final decision in case of dispute, namely, 'Who says?' The claim seems to me to fail to do justice to how it is that human beings and communities actually reach decisions. The notion that what happens is some kind of submission to decisive authority fails to take seriously the fluidity of our handling of ideas and the way our convictions evolve in the light of experience.

That was not the only thing that concerned me in the pattern of argument followed by Packer and others: there seemed to be something odd about God having provided such a 'knockdown' and guaranteed source of authority. The oddness lay in what I felt to be a contrast between that way of providing a foolproof authority and what the Bible itself seems to say about the character of God; does it not jar with Jesus' refusal to compel faith by providing a 'sign' to order, and with the very vulnerability which he manifested in his teaching?

Of course, the debate has moved on dramatically anyway. The conviction that the Bible is the Word of God does not at all prevent us taking seriously all that has been learned by way of biblical criticism. Indeed it has been precisely the strength of the conviction that the Bible contains the Word of God that has led the whole field of the interpretation of Scripture to be opened up in a most creative way. It is striking how much positive affirmation about the biblical message has been produced when Christians whose formation is Evangelical are determined to take on board modern theories of interpretation. It is, after all, considerable evangelical passion as well as critical research that we hear in the words of Bishop John Spong:

> So I hold the Bible before my readers seeking boldly to free it from the clutches of a mindless literalism and, at the same time, presenting it as a dramatic and exciting document whose relevance for our day is both mighty and real. My witness is consistent. I have met the living God in my engagement with Scripture and I have heard the living Word of this God speaking to me through the words of Scripture.[3]

We had moved far from simply seeking to 'explain away' difficult texts or biblical ideas under the pressure of what is assumed to be rational and modern. We have left behind a view of biblical study in which the ultimate ambition was to peel away more and more in the hope of arriving at what could be assumed to be the 'original' tradition. This became very vivid for me in my own researches into the texts about the resurrection of Jesus: the 'detective work' kind of research into 'what happened at the first Easter' opened out into a strong and positive set of discoveries that joined together those first disciples' experiences and the life and witness of the first Christian community, and joined their experience of new life to ours.[4]

That investigation went on alongside working with lay Christians in the discovery of new depths in their faith and how it related to their private and public lives and ministries. That educational work constantly raised the question of authority: what could be learned from the authority that was taken by or ascribed to the educator about the authority that is to be given to the text of the Bible? In the process there opened up for me, in experience as well as in theory, a way of thinking about the question of biblical authority that saves us from having to make the kind of choices among authorities that the traditional debate seemed to require.

There emerged, that is to say, what it could be like for authority and vulnerability to go hand in hand, and for the inner opposition we feel between strength and openness to find some way of being resolved. This is directly relevant to the matter of how we use and regard the Bible. For if it is true, and it seems to me to be true beyond doubt, that the Bible has been used in multiple and conflicting ways. And if it is also true that its emergence as the Bible we now have has been as complex and mysterious as we now know it to have been, does that not in itself tell us something deeply significant about God's dealings with us and our apprehension of God?

That understanding also seems to me to accord much more closely with what we know about how we form our convictions and how they grow and change. For the experience we have of life, of prayer, of the study of Scripture, of engagement and argument with friends and colleagues, is one of movement, revision, dialectic, and certainly not one of submission to one binding authority. The process can sometimes be painful as well as creative; it can involve quite substantial revisions of cherished beliefs. But it is the path of human growth, and the way to mature faith. It gives to biblical authority, not the cringing submission of fearful children, but the attentive seriousness which is what God asks of us in all of our living.

In the intellectual quest for an understanding of the Scriptures, what they are and what they say, I think we have grounds for being immensely excited by the range of insights that have been brought to bear on and have emerged from the reading of the Scriptures. On the one hand, for example within the Evangelical community, there is Anthony Thiselton's formidable gathering together of an immense philosophical literature about interpretation, how it happens and what it is,[5] looking at the whole process by which the reader interacts with the Scripture.

Liberating in quite a different way is the bringing to biblical study of the skills involved in the study of literature. That can help us see the long and complex story of how the Bible emerged, not as a regrettable loss of touch with the original tradition, but as something intrinsic to what the Bible is. So one such scholar, Gabriel Josipovici, can say:

> In the same way the biblical scribes worked within a living tradition, constantly transforming yet always remaining true to the spirit of the whole. Thus the *traces des mains* which are so evident in the Bible should not be seen, as biblical scholarship has always tended to see them, as providing clues to when and where the different elements were written, but rather as a characteristic aspect of its unique being.[6]

Since this is also to be a statement about how these matters appear from the perspective of someone working, as I did until recently, as a bishop, I must add that this movement between how I experience authority and how I understand it in relation to the Bible is profoundly connected with the way authority can be exercised in and by the Church. One of the most important ways in which we as a Christian community can make a statement to the word about God is through the way in which we resolve this issue. We have to find ways of making it clear to each other that we seek ways in which our leaders can be strong because they have made it clear that they are also prepared to be vulnerable. One of the toughest spiritual journeys I found I had to take was the one towards allowing myself to lead *and fail*. It is most often the refusal to run the risk of failure that leads leaders to fail to lead.

One of the most tragic features of the preparation for the debate on the ordination of women was that the bishops as a body, the vast majority of whom believe that women should be ordained, failed to say so corporately. Had they done so they would have taken into themselves the possibility of division and disappointment that the whole Church faces. As it is, our determination as bishops to avoid clear leadership has reduced the respect in which the college of bishops is held and denied to it a real sharing in the pain of the Church and of those for whom the ordination of women is a direct personal issue.

I mention this as an example of the way in which I have found my convictions growing dialectically: as I undergo experience, both private and public, and as it gives me a perception of the challenges of authority, I then study the Scriptures and thereby test that new understanding in the light of what the Bible declares about God and God's people. That in turn changes the way in which I meet new life situations. And this whole movement is undertaken in relation to the Spirit of God known in prayer, worship and the living witness of the Church, increasing my knowledge of the One who both exercises authority over us and at the same time takes huge risks with us.

Supreme among these risks is the emergence of the Bible as a story on the move, and a body of literature whose taking shape and subsequent interpretation bear the marks of so much interplay with human situations and communities. That means there were many false trails, misunderstandings and failures of nerve. The fact that it is human words which are the vehicle of the Word of God makes for uncertainty and even incoherence for those who seek a guaranteed way. But the dialectical engagement of which I have spoken allows us an ever-deepening engagement with God as God has been known in the life of the community of faith and as God was revealed in the one who showed how strength and weakness can be lived out together. It is expressed beautifully in the words of the Roman Catholic scholar Sandra Schneiders, whose recent book on 'interpreting the New Testament as Sacred Scripture' brings together a conviction about the Bible as Word of God and a willingness to trust the way in which it has developed and been interpreted.

For those seeking absolute norms for knowledge and behaviour, [this] position will appear incoherent, unstable, and finally inadequate. For those who realize that the only God worth knowing is a personal God, and that all personal relationships are dialogical and relative, the 'uncontrollability' of God's self-revelation is a source of joyful astonishment and an invitation to the unwavering confidence that only a God of endlessly original love can justify.[7]

To cast such a light on the question of authority in general and its relation to the Bible still leaves unanswered how the Bible and the Church relate to each other. The Bible is, after all, the Church's book; it was produced within and given authority by the community of faith. On that basis it would seem that the Bible remains under the Church's control. On the other hand, the Church has had to submit itself time and again to the judgement of Scripture. The Reformation is one of the supreme examples of how the Bible will have its way when it needs to.

In her account of the Bible as the Church's book, Schneiders likens the relationship of Bible to Church to that between a community and the founding document or constitution that emerges from its original and formative experience. That formative experience comes before the written code, as the community of faith preceded the Bible. But once the experience has been codified the community has to regard itself as subject to it even as it has to interpret it in the light of new experiences and situations.[8]

For all that I have said about the dialectical way in which the Bible has to be interpreted in relation to our experience as individuals and as the Church, I also have to say that I have seen too often what happens when churches fail to root themselves securely enough in the biblical experience. When I have seen the preaching in so-called liberal churches turn into mere chat without any leverage on the life of congregation or members, or when I have observed the exuberance of charismatic worship turn into mere hype without the firmness and direction that are necessary for effective mission, or when Anglo-Catholicism turns into an esoteric and self-indulgent enterprise for the maintaining of customs and practices long after they have ceased to nourish, then mostly it is that the essential dialogue with Scripture has ceased to play its proper part in the life of the community. The constant encounter, by day and by week, with this varied material in all its frequent awkwardness and in all the mysteriousness and untidiness of its development remains for me, though not at all a guarantee, an absolutely necessary safeguard for the Church's integrity.

That dialogue with the Scriptures is also essential in safeguarding the Church from the worst excesses of authoritarian corruption to which it is exposed when it perceives itself as a free-standing institution, in charge of its own way, its own life and its own Scriptures. In fact, the Scriptures are a source of enormous power in the community, not because they have an unchanging and unchallengeable authority, but because of their capacity to continue to call the Church from the corruption of its own pretence to authority, to the service of its essential mission. As Graham Shaw has pointed out:

> Traditionally . . . this power [of the New Testament] has been understood in terms of unchanging authority. The crucial difference, which I am advocating, is that holiness is not a matter of submission to authority, but of exercising freedom. The authoritarian note in scripture, which cannot be ignored, is only a foil to the invitation to freedom, which is its substance.[9]

I have suggested thus far that the Bible responds to the question, 'Who is really in charge – Bible or Church?' first of all by proposing, in its text and in the way it has developed, a different understanding of what it is to be in charge, that it challenges the assumption that what we are to seek is some guarantee of the truth of what we believe and say, that its way of being authoritative challenges many of the ways in which human institutions expect authority to be exercised, and that in its text and in its development it expresses something of how it is that Christians believe God deals with us. I said earlier that I proposed to show that the Scriptures also speak to human beings in their context and in so doing redefine what their context is. It is to that dimension of how I use and regard the Bible that I now want to turn.

For those of us for whom the Bible has been a source of energy and liberation, it is a sobering reflection to think about all the ways in which it has been used during the history of the Church. It has appeared on either side of most of the conflicts of human history, and has without doubt been a tool in the hands of tyrants as often as it has been an instrument of liberation. That contradiction is, of course, as old as the Scriptures themselves. The enormous variety of material contained within our Bible has made it an easy quarry for all who have sought to authenticate whatever course of action or set of convictions they chose to follow.

Reading the Scriptures constitutes an exposure to sublime literature and in the same document to the hate-mail of the ancient world. It is full of prejudices repeated and at the same time of prejudices reformed. It contains what through our eyes can only appear as the worst excesses of nationalism, at the same time as it is a sustained critique of the pretentions of all nations and institutions. There is comfort there for the poor, and comfort for the rich also.

It therefore meets humankind in all sorts of personal and public circumstances, and can be quarried for advice and comfort. Sometimes this seems harmless enough, as when it produces lists like those to be found in the Bibles that the Gideons leave in hotel rooms. But at the same time some of its availability to comfort and affirm human beings in their most oppressive forms of behaviour leaves hearers and readers embarrassed. For however much of the oppressive burden of the use of the Bible can be shown to have come from later interpretation, enough is there in the material itself to make the Bible a very ambiguous piece of literature indeed.

In its variety it invites the reader to deal with the question with which I began. Where do you stand as you look out over the range of material that constitutes the Bible of the Christian Church? What is your real context, and, especially if you have a choice about where you stand, what choice have you made?

I believe that we live at a particularly exciting time in the matter of our response to the Bible because of the emergence of a vast, newly discovered theological resource in the form of interpretations of the Bible by and among people whose context is the outer edge of human society, and who are choosing to dedicate their biblical study to the context in which they find themselves. Most famous among them are the theologians, chiefly from Latin America, who first were given the name of 'theologians of liberation'. But in the wake of their efforts have emerged representatives of particular contexts, committed to the view that the Bible is also for them, and the understanding of it is inherently available to the poor and oppressed of the earth.

Among the most prolific of them have been feminist theologians, who have found that without denying the sexism that is as present in the literature of the Bible as it is in most civilisations, it is possible for them to release the message of liberty and of a new community of women and men that is sometimes open but disregarded, and more often hidden below the surface of the text. Sandra Schneiders' reinterpretation of the encounter between Jesus and the Samaritan woman is a classic of this kind: it reveals the prejudices that have gone into the understanding of that episode in the past as well as being honest about the lurking sexism contained in the body of the text itself.[10]

An investigation of that kind is crucially dependent on where the interpreter is standing. The first decision the interpreter has to make is *from where* is she looking at the text. In this case, Schneiders' decision, like that of many of her sisters, is to look at the Scriptures *as a woman*, and that means as a woman determined to understand the Bible from a position of solidarity with her sisters, in their struggle for a community of women and men.

Similar decisions are being taken by others from their particular contexts. The collection of interpretations of Scripture by

Christians from the Third World edited by R.S. Sugirtharajah[11] is a dramatic case in point. Some of the items in that collection are accounts of bible study groups in Third World settings; some are reinterpretations of texts by scholars, and some are philosophical accounts of what it means to be interpreting the Bible among the poorest of the earth. All of them, and the collection itself, are the products of clarity about where the writers stand. That stance, among the poorest of the world, is a stance 'at the margin', the place from which the writers look at the text. But it is also a stance at the margin in the sense of producing a quite new look, because, as the editor writes:

> To date, biblical interpretation has been exclusively in the hands of male Euro–American scholars. . . . Asians, Latin Americans, Africans, Afro-Americans and Native Americans were excluded both for their concerns and as producers of knowledge. This volume seeks to rectify this imbalance and to introduce exegetical discourse 'from the margin', the work both of those who have had formal exegetical training and of those who have had none.[12]

So these scholars have made a decision to conduct their study of the Bible accepting their context as being at the margin. They note that biblical interpretation has been dominated by those located closest to the centres of power in the world, and rather than seek to accommodate themselves to that setting they are determined to speak out of their context. The emergence of the products of their endeavours, and those of the communities which they serve, so that they are available to Christians in our setting, opens up the possibility of a new kind of interpretation for us as well. We have the possibility of bringing together all that has been learned in the critical study of Scripture and the wealth of experience of those at the margin.[13]

In thinking about this inspiring development over the years, I have found myself facing two questions. First, is such a way of interpreting the Bible in the context of life at the margin actually honest to the nature of the Scriptures themselves? Secondly, how is it that it proves so difficult to achieve in the context in which I find myself, and which I described earlier as that of a white, middle-class English man? That is, in summary, is interpretation 'from the margin' honest to the *text*, and how does it connect with the *subtext* of my own situation?

There is no doubt that the Bible is by no means all written from the margin or for those at the margin. It has within it a full share of the patronising and the domineering, and it has played its full part in the marginalising of excluded groups and individuals. Yet there are, I believe, compelling grounds for saying that it is from that marginal position that the distinctive moments have come when the biblical story has moved creatively forward. Nobody could describe the Bible as wholly a book about peace; it is too full of violence and military endeavour for that. But at the points of decisive onward movement, it is those who speak of or live for God's *shalom* who are found to be offering God's Word. The Bible cannot be called a book about justice: there are too many stories of injustice for it to be right to say that; but yet the key moments of its development have arisen under the impact of those who have put first the reign of God and God's justice.

The truth of the matter is that the concerns of those at the margin are frequently relegated to the margin of the biblical text; their story is often reduced to silence, or they are forced, as in books like Daniel and Revelation, to speak in code, or to leave their needs to be articulated by prophets who were themselves then thrust to the margin through persecution or death. And when the Word of God was acknowledged as appearing in flesh, it too was spoken from the margin in the manner of Jesus' life and his dying.

Those who speak about the Bible from a place at the margin of today's world reflect precisely that dimension of the biblical record. They also have an important comment to make in relation to our question, 'Who is really in charge – Bible or Church?' For they draw our attention to that other 'Church' of the least of Christ's brothers and sisters, to which is also promised the presence of Christ, as Jürgen Moltmann so vividly shows.[14] That other 'Church' will never be 'in charge' in the sense of having power; but it has the moral authority of speaking from the margin of the text of the history of God's people, as the poor and excluded did so frequently in biblical times.

I am therefore in no doubt that those who speak from a place at the margin of society and the world are reflecting a key dimension of the Bible. That brings me to my second question. How is it that this way of thinking about the Bible seems so difficult in the context in which I find myself, that of a white, middle-class English man, and a Church of England bishop? Why is the voice from the margin finding it so hard to make its claim in our country and in our Church?

I will mention just two factors with which I believe we must grapple if we are to discover an engagement that is truly 'from the margins'. In reading Schneiders' account of the relation between the Bible and the Church I was struck by the fact that her ability to say what she does[15] is deeply related to her being part of a nation in which, in experience and constitution, power proceeds upwards from the people, and in a real sense their written laws and constitution are a reflection of the people's desires and experience. Often this is overriden in the interests of those who hold power, but the theoretical basis of their society is that power proceeds from the people.

Ours is the reverse. In our country power proceeds downwards from the sovereign, and the people only have such powers as are conceded to them by the sovereign. The institution of monarchy has been democratised in many ways, but the theory remains intact, buttressed of course by the close relationship between the sovereign and the established Church. Any attempt therefore to produce a biblical interpretation from the margin has to struggle against that deference to the centre which is built into the heart of our national life. For example, it has been possible to put in place, with hardly a murmur of dissent, a structure by which what every child is to learn in school could be decided by one of the Queen's ministers; this is a deeply sinister development, and one which constitutionally could not happen in the USA. I therefore believe that one of the key aspects of the Bible's development, the power of what is in the margin of the text and the presence of God to those who are on the margin of society, is peculiarly difficult for us to understand.

The second factor is one that relates particularly to the Church, and to my experience as a bishop. The pressure to be loyal in the interests of something called 'unity' has to be experienced to be believed. It is deeply embedded within the episcopal heart, and must derive much of its support from tacit expectations within the Christian community. It inhibits most kinds of prophetic utterance and action, unless there is a good likelihood that what is said will command widespread assent.

For such a Church, and such a power structure within it, to hear the Bible through the ears of the marginalised is very hard indeed. It is why there has been a total failure on the bishops' part, as I have already mentioned, to allow a corporate statement of conviction about women's place in the ministry of the Church to emerge; that, despite the fact that the overwhelming majority of them are in favour of the ordination of women. It prevents us again and again from becoming voices for the voiceless.

I was asked to contribute to this series as one of several bishops. I cannot myself see how most of the issues which the Church finds so difficult will be dealt with except under the impact of a serious attempt to see the Bible, and then the issues that face us, from the edge rather than from the perspective provided at the centre. I mentioned early on the feature of our context which is the presence in our nation and world of many other sacred texts, those of the other world faiths. Of course that raises many complex issues for Christians, and a strong intellectual challenge. I am not arguing that thinking about such matters is easy, or that we can lightly abandon stances long held. I am saying that I cannot see how these issues can be addressed other than from a place that really feels what it is to be, as a Muslim, a Sikh or a Jew, always having to struggle for your place at the table of humankind and in the mainstream of British society.

Of course, to take another example, the existence of an increasingly strong and proud gay and lesbian culture is a problem for us, given the long period in which we have been able to assume that their lifestyle was self-evidently wrong. What I am asking is that we attend to the way the Bible itself emerged from the cries of those at the margin. That seems to me to imply that our situation needs to be addressed, not by hitting lesbian and gay people over the head with the six or so available biblical texts, but to go with them, as Christ has been known to go, to their place at the edge, and discover what the world, and the Bible, are like from there.

Of course, there are numerous aspects of our culture which have a long and deep connection with our Christian roots, and of course we have fears when it looks as though we are going to have to be a quite new kind of country, a multi-cultural one, in which not all will accept what we thought were the dominant values. But from whose perspective shall we tackle this, if not from the one provided by those for whom inclusion has proved so hard?

The special concern which bishops are required to have for the outcast and needy is not easy to accommodate within what is also required of them by the institution they serve and whose values they are bound to have taken on board. But mercifully we have the Bible, not just for us to be in charge of, but to engage us with its development and with the vibrant interpretations that emerge from it when it is read from the place where its most creative proclamations were discovered, the edge of the human community. It is, after all, cherished among us as the written inheritance of forebears who described themselves as sinners, saved by a crucified preacher, who was himself rejected by his small occupied nation, who were themselves, often as they may have had to be reminded, descendants of slaves. That should tell us much about its authority and how we should exercise ours.

I offer this as a personal statement of how I use and regard the Bible, and in what sense I hold it to be 'in charge'. The Bible is a book which most of us read at the edge of our working day, and publicly at the edge of our working week. It asks to be taken seriously for the whole of the day and the whole of the week, but its rule is always from the edge. It asks to claim all of our living attention: but because it is the kind of book it is, and has come to us in the way that it has, it can have, if we will let it, a special place in the parts of our lives which we prefer to banish to the margins of our attention, rather as it has a special availability for those at the edge of the human community.

With its rather vulnerable and often abused authority the Bible is, it seems, content. We may long for it to be heard more at the centre of human affairs, but if it were it would too readily become an instrument in the hands of those at the centre of human affairs, as it has so often in the past. We might prefer that it had the kind of authority that would banish our doubts and quell the aspects of our being that seem to alienate us from our ideals and our understanding of what the Bible requires of us. But if it had that kind of authority, again it would banish to the margins of our attention some of our most creative, if disturbing, perceptions.

For these human words are the Word of God for us, but they are the Word of the God we have come to know through the record of God's people, a God who will take risks with us, whose authority will be vulnerable to our error and disobedience, who has chosen to have it that way, and whose Word, therefore, is always 'in character'. And because God is that kind of God who speaks that kind of word, we can know that however far any of God's children may be banished from the centre of human power and human authority, they will not be out of God's hearing and certainly they will not be beyond the scope of God's 'endlessly original love'.

4

GOD'S MESSAGES
AND GOD'S MESSENGERS
David Jenkins

Very soon after my consecration and enthronement, I had a salutary and slightly shaking experience of the effect of becoming a bishop. Or rather, I always put it down to the effects of wearing purple. I believe this is relevant to our theme of the authority and use of the Bible, so I will recount it.

In my capacity as the new diocesan bishop I began by attending all the committees of the diocese of which I was ex officio a member. I hasten to add, I did this once and never again! I had meant just to listen, but at one committee when they went over the same ground for the third time my donnish and managerial heart burst within me. I was moved to comment briefly that surely the following three questions arose, and did it not appear that the possible responses were this, this and that? This innocent contribution to the discussion, designed not to settle the discussion but to move it on, had exactly the opposite effect. It simply stopped the discussion. It took me a little while to realise that the inhibiting element was not me but my purple shirt. The Bishop had said that this was the way in which the matter should be dealt with, so that was that.

From then on I did my best to make it as clear as possible that in a very wide range of contexts, when I – of course as both my personal self and in my representative role of bishop – said something, I was saying it in order to discover, after due discussion and explanation, whether I would or should say it again; and whether it was worth sharing and following up.

Exploration, mutual discussion and investigation are, surely, of the essence of reasonable collaboration, of the taking of responsible and practical decisions and, indeed, of discovering what might be called 'realistic working truths'. Pronouncements do not normally cause people to discover, or to become caught up in and committed to, truths and possibilities which engage and develop them. Being gripped by an apparent truth, and then finding out by response and activity whether or not it is indeed truth and what it means, are much more a matter of process – not pronouncement – and of *shared* process at that.

I start from this point as a bishop invited to reveal publicly how I regard and use Holy Scripture, because it reflects my very personal experiences and wrestlings with how the Bible speaks to me, how I seek to speak responsibly from my reading of the Bible, and how I experience the Bible operating as a source of authority and a resource of inspiration, truth and promise. Although my experience in committee when I came up against what it means to be empurpled in the C of E was not directly about the experience and use of the Bible, it was very sharply about the experience and operation of *authority in community*.

My expectations of the way an authority figure (in this case the bishop) operated within a Christian community (in this case the members of this particular committee within our church synodical structure) were different from the expectations of the rest of my fellow Christians; at least when, so to speak, they were 'in committee' and on their overt and formal behaviour. This, I think, is an important point and an underlying theme of mine throughout what I have to say. It is important because I think that in Christian community and in Christian communities – and not least in the Church of England – we have a strong tendency to produce formal Christian behaviour (including expectations and criticisms based on those expectations) which has very little to do with our actual feelings, responses and behaviour. I did not suppose that the effect of what was taken as my definitive pronouncement would have been very great. In fact all it did, given the overt response to authority, was to stop discussion. Neither did it seem to bring anything in the longer run. I had more experience of this as I gradually became better known as a bishop and more familiar with the set-up. For instance, experiences around the diocese of people listening to me – say at a Pastoral Committee – and then saying: 'well, Bishop, tell us what we ought to do.' And that, of course, is fatal. People do not actually want to be told; they want to be able to criticise people who make pronouncements.

I hope you do not think this is trivial; I am trying to speak about authority, the use of the Bible, and other things, from ordinary experience. For the moment we can leave on one side the issue of the effectiveness of authority and of authorities, and concentrate on the issue of the expectation of authority and authorities.

I think that there can be no doubt that that rather trifling personal encounter of mine with the issue of authority in a Christian community accurately reflected the normative (and normal) public and shared expectation of authority and of authorities in Christian communities at large. That is to say, the normal expectation is one of authoritative pronouncements. I may say that one of the things we experience in the House of Bishops is all sorts of people who want us to make all sorts of statements about all sorts of things. The expectation is of pronouncements uttered by recognised authorities on the basis of a recognised authority. This is the model and expectation, whether the basic authority is held to be the Church, the Bible or a *testimonium internum spiritus sancti* (the internally given witness of the Holy Spirit) – all different models which actually separate people into parties; yet all are actually basically the same model. We may compare, for the Church, the famous '*Roma locuta causa finita*' (Rome has spoken, the matter is definitively settled). We are surely also familiar with 'This cannot be done' (or considered, or believed) 'because the Bible says' so and so. We have all met individuals – have we not? – who say, with evident conviction: 'God has told me.' Whenever anyone says that to me I remember the famous story about Bishop Montgomery-Massingbird who met an ordinand slipping away from a retreat when he was not supposed to. The ordinand said: 'I am sorry, Bishop, but the Holy Spirit has told me to buy my wife a present.' And the Bishop replied, 'Well, it is a pity that the Holy Spirit didn't tell you it is early closing day.'

This, therefore, is the assumption: that there are authoritative sources which are directly available to enable and empower, directly applicable, authoritative pronouncements. Now, my existential and experiential position – which I believe I can strongly support logically, morally and theologically – is that things are simply not like that. There are no pronouncements of unquestionable authority and absolutely obvious meaning which come directly to us from God, or unerringly put us directly on to God.

Almost all of us who are Christian believers really know in our heart of hearts that this is so, but we have not so far found the common conviction and the common language to put it clearly, simply and convincingly. We appear to be unsure and unsettled about the authenticity and glory of our faith and to be at sixes and sevens among ourselves about the basic simplicity of the glory and gospel of God, while we discuss endless detail. So, for instance, every new book pointing out critical difficulties about the New Testament (most of which have been known to any one who has known anything for years and years and years) is taken to be one more nail in the coffin of an obsolescent, fading and superstitious faith which has less and less credible claim to be based in a set of saving, promising and revealing encounters with God. I have had all sorts of people ringing me up about the latest four or five books, and I have had to explain patiently how all these points have come up before and that we have been living with them for years.

Now this is deeply sad as far as a deeply confused and lost world goes; alarmingly faithless and self-centred, it seems to me, as far as our Christian responsibilities go; and, surely, unnecessary. For – if I may say so – if the Bible is anything to go by, God is powerful *in the midst*. God is not an answer to particular questions, but a constant resource, a constant experience, a constant promise in the midst of all these things.

Within the churches we seem to have become fixated on words and to have lost the inspiration, vision and challenge of the Word. We seem to have lost our grip on the Word by which God created the heavens and the earth, and which became the Word made flesh. This Word is the very intimate, actual, expression of God's being, purpose, and promise: God expressing himself and sharing himself. God is Love. So this Word can encompass the whole of creation and be simply a person in and as Jesus in all his vulnerability. Then we can go on to understand that the availability of the creative and redeeming work of God's Word is carried on by the Spirit into the intimacy of personal lives and the immanent possibilities of the world. This is the Spirit which, as the Holy Spirit of God, is the Spirit of the risen Jesus Christ, who is the Incarnate Word of God.

All this can be pointed to, but cannot be contained within, words. It is no wonder, therefore, that the wonder and mystery of God can neither be directly described nor unerringly encountered by means of pronouncemens. God is discovered, encountered and received among people, through processes of exploration, experiment, rescuing and renewal, and in pilgrimmage and presence. This, surely, is what the Bible is about, what the Bible portrays and how the Bible works.

In order that I may remain an existential and as personal as possible in this consideration of the use of Holy Scripture, I would like to go on exploring the points and possibilities I have so far raised by asking: 'What is the use of the Bible?'

I ask this quite seriously, and with reference to some of our immediately pressing Christian controversies. If we imagine that the use of the Bible is to settle authoritatively such controversies, then surely it is obvious that the Bible is not of much use. What we are confronted with in practice is a contradictory and contested use of the Bible. Take for example the ordination of women to the priesthood.

There is, for example, a group from among the Evangelical tradition, or traditions, who say that what Paul has to say about headship simply, decisively and permanently rules out the ordination of women to the authoritative office of priesthood. I set on one side what that actually says about the understanding of the authority of the priesthood (although that, I suspect, is an example of the way in which people who tell us what the Bible means very often tell us more about themselves than about the Bible). By no means all people who claim to be Evangelicals accept this argument; and to many others the argument is simply not credible. It is pointed out that Paul also says that in Christ there is neither male nor female, Jew nor Greek, bond nor free. To which, of course, the arguers reply: but that applies to baptism, not priesthood.

Now the question is: how do we know? How do we know definitively and in a God-guaranteed way? In any case, many deep believers and careful students of the Bible go on to say that Paul's texts about women are so conditioned by context and culture that to use them in this definitive way is simply to misunderstand and misapply. And so it goes on. Once you begin to look into the arguments, as I have already indicated, a Pauline pronouncement like any other has first to be picked out as centrally relevant to our issue, next has to be interpreted, and then applied.

Once one starts to look into matters of context and acceptance, interpretation and application, it becomes pretty clear that very few sets of words indeed have a meaning, interpretation and application about which everyone would obviously agree on simple hearing of the words. This, surely, is part of the problem. Words, you see, can be taken in a variety of ways.

Consider, also, our present very real and disturbing differences and difficulties about homosexuality. Now it seems to me clear that what few biblical texts there are that apply directly to homosexual practices are negative and condemnatory – by their language usage and in their context. This is taken by some people to be decisive. But there is a growing body of argument which refuses to accept this. First, there is the issue of cultural conditioning. Secondly, there is the issue of a developing understanding of the 'natural' variations of human sexuality across its whole spectrum. Thirdly there is, for instance, the issue of a generally growing understanding of the lives and attitudes of the substantial numbers of persons who find themselves to be homosexual – this includes the issue of their persecution by attitudes sustained within both the Church and society at large.

Can a few texts settle such a complex human matter? In practice many responsible Christians deny this. At a deeper level – in a way – in theory and theology, is this selective textual approach a proper and faithful way to regard and use the Bible?

While we are on this point, a brief reference may also be made to divorce. A bishop in the Church of England must be particularly aware of the almost daily difficulties which arise with regard to particular cases of marriages involving divorced persons. This is very much a practical matter. It is not easy to maintain in practice, with both simplicity and clarity, a clear witness to the Christian view of marriage (as intended to be a place and opportunity of a life-long commitment between two mutually committed persons) and also a witness to the Christian understanding of the forgiveness and renewal of God in relation to sinful, mistaken and repentant persons. Now, both of those approaches – about marriage and about forgiveness and renewal – would seem to me to be profoundly biblical insights; that is to say, to fit into the whole thrust and pattern of the Bible about God, human beings, his purposes for them and his graciousness to them. But in practice as a bishop I cannot get formal and simple agreement on how to witness to this because, among other things, the legislative bodies of our Church cannot agree a common way of presenting and practising these two, surely highly complementary, understandings and insights. And here is the rub: a principal reason for this is a disagreement about the bearing and application of one text, and perhaps a couple more, in the Gospels. What is the use of the Bible here?

I am not, of course, supposing for one minute that my preceding paragraphs have adequately dealt with any of the complex and controverted matters of the ordination of women to the priesthood, of homosexuality, or of approaches and practices with regard to the marriage of divorced persons – although we are all wrestling with all these matters. I am simply pointing to the incontrovertible fact that within the Church the Bible seems to be used more to prevent agreement than to promote it. The Bible may contain sufficient reference to all things generally necessary to salvation, but we do not seem to be able to use it easily, effectively and consensually for anything in particular; especially when the particulars trouble us (or some of us) at some awkward personal, psychological or social level.

Here, as part of realism and practicality, it is probably useful to point out that there are other areas than the directly sexual and familial ones where we do not seem to be nearly so overtly and deeply troubled by disagreements over the use and application of the Bible. For instance, it has always seemed to me that many New Testament texts (not least many in the Sermon on the Mount) make on the face of it an exceedingly strong case for Christian pacifism. Yet pacifism has always remained a very minority conviction in the Church and people do not hurl texts at one another, either anxiously or angrily, on the subject. There is also the fact that there are probably as many texts in the Books of Moses which oppose usury as there are ones concerned with homosexuality. Indeed, the Bible at large is pretty severe about rich people and unjust commercial and social dealings. But political arguments about Christian approaches to money, banking and financial markets are rarely confused (or should it be 'enlightened'?) by passionate and frequent use of biblical texts.

Now since I have been asked to speak personally from my experience and practice as a Christian disciple who has for nine years now been a diocesan bishop, I am bound to say that my impression and conclusion is that the passionate and controversial use of biblical texts is almost entirely defensive and an expression of anxiety, fear and uncertainty. From a pastoral and from a missionary point of view, it seems to me that our refusal to be clear-sighted about how we actually use the Bible, at least in public controversy and in attempts which are allegedly about coming to a common Christian mind, is a prime example of the way we Christians kid ourselves. We kid ourselves about what we do and how we do it. We deceive ourselves about our actual behaviour and we obscure the wealth and resource of the Bible, because it is clearly used to be awkward, by troubled and often neurotic people. Our public use of the Bible as allegedly authoritative, continually demonstrates that its authority is very ineffective indeed. It is plain that the Bible settles nothing for us – at least, once we have got into an argument or an anxiety, an uncertainty, about something which we regard as being of human, spiritual and social importance.

My conclusion is that in too much practice we have simply allowed ourselves to misplace and mistake the authority and use of the Bible. Here I can only point in the direction which I believe to be true, practical and powerful about the authority of the Bible, by giving a brief testimony. The arguments that lead up to it, and the arguments that follow from it, have to be left unsaid.

I was introduced to the authority and power of the Bible by persons. They were persons who invited me to join with them in relating the Bible to my life, their life, and God's offer. We worked at this through Bible classes. The people who conducted these Bible classes were also people who either preached to me, or invited other people to preach to me, from – as they believed – the Bible. My experience was that these were lively, committed and convincing persons who pointed me, through their own use and experience of the Bible and their fellowship around it, to a God who cared for me. They found this God spoken of, and reflected in, stories and other literature in the Bible and they saw him especially focused, defined and offered in Jesus, around whom, in the name of God, the stories, writings and wrestlings of the New Testament were especially focused. I began to share their convictions, their commitment and, I must stress, their searchings. For from the beginning my introduction to the Bible offered me a sense of search, excitement, investigation, questioning and indeed controversy (what does this *mean*?). But it was controversy within a shared fellowship, commitment and expectation. We wanted to find out what God would show us through our study and searching of the Bible as we did it with one another.

I stress this because I must make it clear that it was before I came to any detailed critical study of biblical texts, or of the biblical literature in its historical context, that I learned to question biblical texts as a serious and necessary part of taking the Bible seriously as a resource, an inspiration and an authority. That has stayed with me to this day – and sometimes it nearly catches me out, as on those days when I have left my sermon a little late on a Saturday, and discover that the people who chose what they thought was a better version for the Alternative Service Book have landed us on a certain Sunday with an absolutely incredible short text from Paul which is just unbelievably obscure. The only thing to do then is simply to sit down in front of it and start cross-referencing, see what other bits of the Bible will say about this particular bit, and vice versa. The process is perfectly simple, sometimes quite difficult, but – I am bound to say – I think never, in my experience, ineffective.

From this initial set of experiences onwards I have found my experience and use of the Bible a steadily enlarging one. I have found that the Bible, in a multiplicity of ways, is the story, not of course, of a God who was simply for me or even for 'us' – but of a God who was the God of all and for all. And this story has in it all sorts of wrestlings – for instance about unsettled interaction between particular persons and particular called groups, and the wider groupings of mankind and the ongoing developments of history (the minor prophet Joel comes immediately to mind). There are plenty of wrestlings within the Bible. Indeed, as I went on I discovered – with the help of teachers, traditions, theology and worship – that the God reflected in the Bible, through the experiences, stories and prayers of those who were the subject of his revealing encounters, was the God who was concerned as mysterious and total Love to share himself with the whole of creation and who was at work to redeem and fulfil to that end.

Thus the Bible became for me, and continues to develop for me, as an inexhaustible resource of inspiration, insight, correction and encouragement. I learned to enter into all this through persons. I shall continue to pursue all this with persons, and as I do so I am incorporated into the personal workings of the God who goes beyond all understanding, but who is always catching us up into his caring and works, his correction and his creation.

I fear that this testimony is totally inadequate, but I hope at least it shows why I gave the title of my contribution to this series as 'God's Messages and God's Messengers'. The Bible came alive for me through messengers of God's gospel who pointed me to messages available to me. As I learned gradually, and am still learning, these are messages which are available to all. The Bible is itself an immense compilation of messages, stories, prayers, wrestlings and challenges which has been put together by messengers about the messages they have received. Its use lies always within the pilgrim peoples of God, who go on seeking to live by, and to live out, these messages. So the messengers themselves become part of the ongoing message of the love and Kingdom of God. We are ourselves called to be messengers by the very nature of the messages we receive, along with our fellow messengers and pilgrims.

This came into my mind in particular early in my episcopate when St Michael and All Angels fell on a Sunday. I had preached on angels. Having pointed out first of all that as far as angels went they needed demythologizing because they hadn't the necessary bosoms to harbour the muscles needed to flap their wings to fly, we then got on to the business about *angelos* and messengers, and people being messengers and people therefore probably being angels. At the coffee afterwards one of the gentlemen present said to me: 'Oh I am not bothered about you now, Bishop. I see what you are, you are just a teaching vicar. You are explaining things.' This, of course, was a great grace to be given to me at that particular time. It is by unpacking and by expounding, by asking questions about and by sharing, that the message is repeated. You cannot separate Bible and people. You cannot set the Bible as a verbal authority over against the people who live by the Bible.

This does not leave us at the mercy of pure subjectivity, because of a whole series of things. For instance, the Bible is *there*. It can mean all sorts of things but it cannot mean everything and so mean nothing. It has to be taken very seriously indeed. It must be wrestled with and studied. One part must be compared with another, and you must give a reasoned account to other people of what you get out of it.

Secondly, we have built up a great tradition of experience and a great experience of tradition. God has continued with his messages and his messengers. Without the long experience of encounter with God and encounters with his world, tradition can solidify, become trapped and suffocate – just as biblical texts can. But used in an open way, tradition is a vital resource for preserving and reminding us of the central biblical insights and hopes and our responsibilities. (Our forefathers in the faith made *this* of it and it made *this* of them, so we must pay attention to this past.) The tradition, continuity in the tradition, and listening to the tradition, arguing with the tradition and giving answer to the tradition – these are an essential part of taking the Bible seriously.

Thirdly, we have the responsibility and opportunity of being accountable to one another about our developing faithfulness to the God of the Bible. Patterns of response and discovery have to be worked out in mutual, hopeful, and faithful accountability to one another. That is why dialogue, conversation, investigation, exploration and even controversy, are so important. *My* faith has to be worked out as part of *our* faith. The continuing messengers are responsible under God, through one another and to one another, for the faithfulness, continuity and authenticity of the message.

And finally – and this is the basis of it all, is it not? God is not a deliverer of revelations past. His is the sustainer of revelations present. We are promised and given the Spirit – the Spirit whom I have come to see more and more is, I believe, God wrestling with his creative risks and our human and often sinful mistakes.

Just as God in Christ was incarnate in order to enter fully into the sinfulness, desolation, corruption and death which has overtaken the creation; so this involvement, this continual wrestling and suffering is, I believe, continued in the Spirit. God in the Spirit is bearing the cost of his own risk of setting us free (so that we have to choose, and take part and collaborate and be able to make a mess of things); God is exercising his creative risk by sharing in our human and often sinful mistakes. We are not left on our own. We have a share in the Spirit.

And this I think, is highly relevant to any vote in General Synod – for instance, on the ordination of women. The result of a vote is not necessarily the will of God; it is the statistical accident arising out of the way numbers of people have moved their feet. The question is, how then do we collaborate with the Spirit of God to make something about his Kingdom out of it? This surely has always been the case: 'As the Churches of Jerusalem and Antioch hath erred, so hath the Church of Rome' – in which case, so certainly, many times, has the Church of England! To think otherwise is a failure to understand the Spirit and a conceit on our part about being directly influenced by God with no possibility of error. We cannot avoid the responsibility of collaboration and we take our responsibility in total dependence on the mercy of God. We have to choose as honestly and faithfully as we can, and then we have to look for forgiveness and newness and collaboration. I simply do not believe that anyone can dare to say that the result of a vote in Synod is directly the will of God. We may be part of the will of God or we may make things worse; it depends on how we go on. This has become clearer and clearer to me; I personally could not tolerate the Church else. Look at the things the Church has done down through history! Look at what people have done on the basis of biblical authority! Unless there is a gap in which God risks our collaboration and then, mercifully and graciously, and in collaboration with us – in our stumbling, humility and humiliation – brings his purposes out of it, then there can only be hell to pay.

We have to be clear that God risks our personal responsibility and collaboration. We must go through with our anxieties and inadequacy about the use of the Bible and the living out of God's purposes. But God is there – as the Bible makes clear again, and again and again. God is there – working gradually, perseveringly, patiently and, I must believe, suffering amid it all. He is there to continue to shape us, lead us, persuade us, correct us and entice us, so that we can continue to be his messengers – both receiving and passing on his messages. In particular we must help one another out of any idolatry of words; of any idolatry of sheer textual forms – forms which, however, have been, and of course can be, vehicles, indicators, triggers of messages. Arguing by texts is worse than useless. It is a betrayal of personal responsibility and insight and a travesty of God. The Living Lord, Logos and Spirit is often, it seems to me, downgraded by our use of texts as if he were some sort of heavenly computer who churns out celestial printouts. (Even then we don't seem to be able to read the print very well!) Clearly, this is a complete travesty of the way God is experienced and reflected in the Bible. (It has become clearer and clearer to me that so many uses of the Bible simply are not biblical.) The Bible is an account of people wrestling mostly *without* texts about the continuity of the life of the people of God in relation to being told about betrayals of the past, uncertainties present and futures hidden. The way we can, and must, live from the Bible and with the Bible is from within the community of those who are called to be part of God's ongoing life and message and purpose of creation, salvation and fulfilment.

That is why, as a practising bishop, I remain convinced that even the Church cannot keep a good God down. It is quite clear to me that although one can so rarely do with the Church, we simply cannot do without it. Unless you have the People, the Book will mean nothing. Nevertheless, this does not mean we can avoid facing the fact that the way the People behave very often makes the Book incredible. The responsibility is ours – under God and through the Spirit; and we can face this responsibility because the God who is portrayed in the Bible is infinitely patient, infinitely forgiving – although also necessarily judgemental.

In closing I add this. One of the things I have discovered (it all arose out of studying certain Pauline texts and epistles with certain other text) is that we cannot possibly face up to what the Bible says about God and his love unless we face up to what the Bible says about wrath. Love cannot abide that which is against it. This is why, in 1 Thessalonians, for instance, I am reminded of the primitive Christian gospel, which was that Jesus, who had been shown to be the Christ of God by the resurrection from the dead, will deliver us from the wrath to come. If God is making an End to his purposes of love, then of course he must clear up. Yet, I was reminded that the Judge is the Saviour – they are one and the same person. Therefore one can be quite clear that there is always hope in facing judgement, for the purpose for which God judges is that we may repent and be saved. Somehow one has got to get back to this immense sternness – which is, however, the sternness of Love and the hope of redemption. This may be obvious to you; it came to me out of simple study of the texts for other purposes. There is an authenticity and power about the texts which is there to correct us, but our personal responsibility remains.

In short, we have the Bible, we may use the Bible and we can rejoice and rest in the Bible because (if I may so sum it up) God is not a dictating God. God, as he has shown in Jesus Christ, is neither dictating nor a dictator. The Word became flesh. Everything turns on personal and embodied messages, suffering and resurrection. The Bible portrays a God of great mystery and absolutely persevering Love, who from the Mystery beyond personality is personally involved in communication, commitment, creation and redemption. We can only share in the authoritative hearing and the authoritative passing on of the Bible as we also become together pilgrims, receivers of messages, and also messengers in the creative pilgrimage which is the pilgrimage of this biblical and universal God.

5

PRAYER AND
THE SCRIPTURES
David Hope

Some time ago a friend of mine came to see me, and in the course of our conversation she said that she had just returned from a retreat. I inquired about the addresses – had they been helpful? Had they been instructive? Had they been useful? 'Oh,' she replied, 'there were no addresses.' 'Were you then in silence the whole time?' 'Oh, yes,' came the answer, 'but we had our daily Scripture verses given us individually by the conductor.' As our conversation continued, it emerged that this was a totally new experience for my friend. Never before had she been on a retreat of this nature, where just one verse of Scripture was the nourishment, the spiritual food, day by day.

It took me back to the time when I was training for ordination, and the retreat during Holy Week which was a particular feature of the course. Everyone was expected to do this once in their training period – and having done it, I have to say that once was quite enough for me! But I still have the small green notebook in which, again, a verse of Scripture was given, for example Isaiah 53.5: 'He was wounded for our transgressions, he was bruised for our iniquities; upon him was the chastisement that made us whole, and with his stripes we are healed'; or Romans 6.4: 'We were buried therefore with him by baptism into death, so that as Christ was raised from the dead by the glory of the Father, we too might walk in newness of life.' There was a twenty-minute exposition of the particular verse and then you were left to complete the remainder of the hour-long period of meditation reflecting for yourself on the verse, its more immediate application to you, your situation and circumstances, as you, together with others around you, journeyed with the Lord through the events of his saving passion, death and resurrection.

Now there are, I suppose, few homes in which you will not find a copy of the Bible somewhere, even if it is a dusty copy of the Authorised Version handed down from generation to generation. Thanks to the Gideons, most hotel rooms offer, among all the other facilities, a copy of the Scriptures. But all too often the Bible remains on the bookshelf or in the bedside cabinet. Indeed, one of my very clear childhood memories is of two copies, beautifully bound, of Philip Lord Wharton Bibles in the glass cabinet in our front room. The front room was the posh room, reserved only for Sundays and Christmas and Easter, and for receiving particularly special people – and, I well remember also, the room where my grandmother was laid out! For the rest of the time we were in the back all-service living room. The Philip Lord Wharton Bibles were occasionally taken out of the glass cabinet, but only very occasionally. For the most part they had been put on one side.

Prayer, and the reading of Scripture, have for many of us been put to one side. Many may remember from childhood the nightly pattern of prayer instilled in us by parents, kneeling at the foot of our beds, struggling to stay awake as we prayed for sick relatives and pets as well as 'God bless mummy, God bless daddy', and so on. Today, 'God help us' is a phrase found on the lips of many people, uttered more as an expletive than as a genuine cry for help. More than ever before, the unique contribution to the quality of our lives that prayer and the Scriptures afford needs to be recognised. However, there is something of a dilemma here for the present-day disciple of Jesus Christ. For the separation of Scripture and prayer has been made all the more acute by the development of modern critical study of the Bible. The contemporary Christian is confronted with the difficulty of seeking to bring the insights of critical scholarship to bear upon the texts, while at the same time trying to retain a relationship with the Scriptures that allows them to be proper and effective channels of God's word and God's grace.

This process of recovering the Scriptures to assist us in our earthly pilgrimage began at the Reformation. Until 1536, possession of an English Bible could lead you to the bonfire. Translation into the vernacular generated a new thirst for the Scriptures, and from 1538 the Great Bible was ordered to be set up in every parish church.

In 1542 one of my predecessors in the see of London, Edmund Bonner, ordered every priest in the diocese to study one chapter of the New Testament each week and learn the passage by heart. Literate laity soon caught on, and the demand became so great that the government had to set cost controls.

Bible-reading became important for devotions of the clergy. The 1549 Book of Common Prayer required all clergy to say Morning and Evening Prayer daily. In the course of a year the whole Old Testament was read once and New Testament three times. The intention of this scheme of ordering the Scriptures is quite plainly set out in Cranmer's Introduction to The Book of Common Prayer – 'Concerning the Service of the Church':

> that the Clergy, and especially such as were Ministers in the congregation, should (by often reading and meditation in God's Word) be stirred up to godliness themselves, and be more able to exhort others by wholesome doctrine, and to confute them that were adversaries to the truth; and further that the people (by daily hearing of Holy Scripture read in the Church) might continually profit more and more in the knowledge of God and be the more inflamed with the love of his true religion.

So there is a double intention here – first of all for the clergy that they should be faithful to the vows made before the bishop in ordination ('Will you be diligent in Prayers and in the reading of the holy Scriptures and in such studies as help to the knowledge of the same, laying aside the study of the world and the flesh . . . Will you be diligent to frame and fashion your own

selves and your families according to the Doctrine of Christ . . .'
and so on), and also in the same Introduction for the people (and
the implication here is that they will be daily hearing the reading
of God's Word), that they may 'continually profit more and
more in the knowledge of God and be the more inflamed with
the love of his true religion'.

And here at once is, I believe, a very good and necessary and
vital connection between public worship and personal prayer –
the way the one echoes and complements the other, the way the
one feeds and nourishes and supports and sustains the other. I
fear that, with an increasing variety of types and styles of services
and language in our Church of England, we are in danger of
losing that cohesiveness which I believe to be truly a vital element of who and what we are as members together in one
Church. The words, the phrases – for example, the collects for
Advent, for Ash Wednesday and so on – repeated as they were
Sunday after Sunday, day after day, became a part of the individual's own personal prayer; they became deep-down things, the
prayer of the individual caught up in the prayer of the whole
Church, and vice versa.

Of course, the most obvious way the Scriptures have influenced prayer has been from the very beginning in prayer made
in the public domain. The Lord's Prayer as set out by the evangelists has always had a place of primacy and privilege. And as
the Eucharist began to emerge as the main Sunday Service in the
various Christian communities, the Eucharistic Prayer, itself reflecting the framework of the Jewish blessing over meals, began
to pick up the biblical themes of creation, redemption and new
life in Christ, at the heart of which is the narrative of the Last
Supper. The early formal prayers of the Eucharist, as they are
collected together in the Verona manuscript known generally as
the Leonine Sacramentary, show that whilst on the whole the
formal liturgical prayer of the Church did not generally incorporate actual quotations from Scripture, nevertheless phrases, allusions, echoes of scriptural passages, are very evident.
Occasionally, and particularly in situations where there is

considerable conflict, Scripture is actually enlisted in the onslaught against adversaries in their denunciation.

So far as the public worship of our own Church is concerned, the daily offices of Morning and Evening Prayer, as well as the Scripture readings, incorporate more formally as canticles other passages of Scripture – *Magnificat, Benedictus, Jubilate Deo*, and so on. Indeed, in more recent times biblical canticles have abounded; there are numerous of them in circulation at the present time. Other 'prayers' to be found in the Bible are often incorporated into special services, and here I think particularly of the dedication or consecration of a church or chapel, where considerable use is made, for example, of the prayer of King Solomon (1 Kings 8.22ff). There can be no doubt of the strong scriptural basis and content of the formal public prayer of our Church, and that was plainly and clearly set out by Cranmer in the Introduction to The Book of Common Prayer to which I have already referred.

Today, access to the texts in our own language has been made possible by the efforts of Bible translators across the world. The challenge, however, for the contemporary Christian is to see how modern theological enquiry and its questions about authenticity of texts need not undermine our ability to hear the very word of the Lord speaking to us through the Scriptures.

Throughout the centuries of Christian tradition, many Christians have used the Bible as a significant stimulus to their own prayer and devotion. The monastic tradition of *lectio divina* required monks to read Scripture in order to memorise it and learn it by heart, to 'chew' and 'masticate' its contents in their minds so as to provide fuel for the heart to pray and the will to do God's will in the common round and daily task. Meditation of this kind relied on an implicit confidence in the Scriptures as God's written word for his Church and world.

Such confidence underlies the great spiritual classics of the Christian tradition. *The Dark Night of the Soul* of St John of the Cross and *The Interior Castle* of St Teresa of Avila are examples of spiritual writing that depend on a wrestling and struggling with

Scripture as a source of divine inspiration. And here I am reminded particularly of the approach of one of my personal favourites – Aelred, Abbot of Rievaulx in the twelfth century. Already I have mentioned the phrase *lectio divina* with regard to the Scriptures. It seems to me that it is perfectly proper to wrestle with the exegetical and critical questions which the Scriptures present – that these should not be evaded or avoided, but rather struggled with in an exciting and expectant way, rather than getting on with the task simply because it is there to be pursued. But I do believe that this enterprise is to be pursued in the complementary context of the use of Scripture in public worship and personal prayer, and to this end *lectio divina* – the use of Scripture as a means of forming the heart and mind, as a way of putting on Christ – is an equally important and legitimate pursuit alongside the scholarly and critical study of the Scriptures. Indeed, the one without the other will undoubtedly lead to a misshapen view. The one with the other will ensure something of a struggle as well as a proper balance; but then faith, if it is anything, is always something of a struggle in which, though now we see through a glass darkly, then we shall see face to face.

Aelred exemplifies the monastic quest, and there can be no doubt whatever that any reading of the works of the medieval monks demonstrates their amazing and extensive familiarity with the Scriptures. But as one writer describes it, 'the monk's primary concern in reading the Word of God was not to satisfy his intellectual curiosity but to stimulate his quest for God'. 'Fervour, not questions, is your quest; incitement to charity, not subtlety of argument,' was Aelred's instruction to his monks. Indeed, the men and women of the Bible became his friends, such was the degree of his familiarity with the Scriptures. Again, another writer, St Bernard, sums up well the practice of *lectio divina*. 'In monastic theology *lectio divina* is not simply an intellectual exercise, but a communing with the living God who reveals himself to us through His Word. It is the occasion of a visit from the Lord, a reading with God in His company, with His help a reading that involves two.' This spiritual exercise is accompanied by a relish which, surpassing a mere notional knowledge, leads to a true religious experience suited to each individual. This light which comes from the inspired text (it is important to note) on the occasion of the *lectio*, is received by the soul as a personal message, which is meant for it and serves to build up its faith. The monk of the middle ages was not primarily interested in the letter of the text, as is the exegete of today, but in the profit he could draw from it for his spiritual life. The purpose of the *lectio* was to stimulate devotion: 'Whatever is fittingly suggested by these holy pages, to rouse faith, strengthen hope, set charity aflame, be sure the Holy Spirit has both hidden it there and discovered it to you,' writes another.

And such a sentiment would, I believe, be equally true for today. The regular and ordered and, yes, disciplined reading of the Holy Scriptures ought as much as anything to be towards this stimulation of devotion, so that truly the mind of Christ can be formed in us. In a quite different context Barnabas Lindars speaks of 'the biblical formation of the mind'. Well, for any Christian disciple there is the biblical formation of our whole lives, and a primary feature in and for such a life is the way in which a reflective and prayerful reading of the Scriptures – perhaps simply dwelling upon, resting upon, a verse of two for some considerable time – opens the heart and mind in prayer.

In modern times, Vatican II, and in particular the Dogmatic Constitution on Divine Revelation, has insisted on the trustworthiness of Scripture as an inspired and authoritative work of God:

> Since the Scriptures are inspired by God and committed to writing once and for all time, they present God's own word in unalterable form, and they make the voice of the Holy Spirit sound again and again in the words of the prophets and apostles. It follows that all the preaching of the Church, as indeed the entire Christian religion, should be nourished and ruled by sacred Scripture . . . such is the force and power of the Word of God that it can serve the Church as her support

and vigour, and the children of the Church as strength for their faith, food for the soul, and a pure and lasting fount of spiritual life.[1]

To pray and meditate upon the Scriptures, then, is to open the door into the presence of God through Jesus Christ by way of the sacred texts. As André Louf has written, with particular reference to the Psalms: 'The Spirit in which Jesus prayed and recreated the psalms is poured out on every baptized person, who in the same Spirit can now, like Jesus, make the psalm his/her own and pray it anew.'[2]

André Louf is himself, of course, formed in the monastic tradition, which has at its heart the daily and regular recitation of the Psalter. How many of us fall back on such well-known psalms to frame our prayer when there are no words of our own with which to pray – The Twenty-Third Psalm, for example, expresses so much which seems quite inexpressible in our own words, and yet puts into words thoughts that do 'lie too deep for tears'. One of my most impressive experiences during a visit in 1991 to the Romanian convent of Varatec in Moldavia, was the way in which there was a constant recitation of the Psalter throughout the day and throughout the night. In that place of some two hundred or so nuns, at least a dozen were constantly within the church chanting the Psalter. And why? Well, precisely for the reasons which Louf states. Furthermore, Thomas Merton in his *Bread in the Wilderness* speaks very powerfully of the way in which the individual, and the Church as a whole, is caught up in the 'I' of the psalmist. Merton writes:

> The kings of strange desert tribes have survived in the psalms; they were the enemies of Israel. Their mysterious names do not mean anything definite to us. These kings emerged from the verses of psalms like the weird symbolic enemies that menace us in dreams and fade away. They are the powers of evil that are still around us today. We know that Sisera is dead with a tent peg in his temple, and Jabin's bones long ago whitened in the ravine of Cisson. Yet Jabin and Sisera still rise

up to plague us though they cannot prevail. But we know, on the nights when their names pass before us, in the small hours, at the chanting of Mattins, that the old battles we are celebrating are more than ever actual. Actual too are the same miracles by which Israel overcame her enemies and entered glorious through divided Jordan to occupy the Promised Land. These battles and these victories go on without ceasing, generation after generation and century by century, because the whole church is still passing out of Egypt, company by company. The shining tribes of Israel are still crossing the desert in the slow indeterminable march that Baalam saw from his mountain when his curse against them choked in his gullet and turned into a song of praise.[3]

Throughout the Bible the encouragement to prayer is writ large. The conviction that God hears prayer and is moved by prayer underlies every page. In the Old Testament it is made clear that, whilst all have access to God in prayer, nevertheless God has appointed those who represent his people to him and him to the people. The Old Testament knows of two modes of such appointment: priestly and prophetic. Aaron and his line are appointed in the priestly way. Prophets are appointed by the direct anointing of the Holy Spirit, and they are authorised to speak to God almost face to face and to take part in his council, by receiving from him a share in his own spirit (Exodus 33.11; Jeremiah 23.18). The outstanding people of prayer in the Old Testament are all prophets. Moses is the great intercessor, and later Judaism also singled out Jeremiah. Of Abraham it is specifically stated, in connection with the plight of Abimelech: 'He is a prophet and he will pray for you' (Genesis 20.7).

It is usually only by hindsight that true prophets can be clearly distinguished from false ones (Deuteronomy 18.22), and we shall often only see long afterwards that some of our prayers really were from God, while others, that we felt absolutely sure of at the time, fell very wide of the mark. And it is not only our weakness that may come between our praying and the ends we hoped for. In the Old Testament, the prophet, inspired and prompted by God's own Spirit, takes part in God's council to such a degree that God is sometimes said to 'change his mind' (Exodus 32.14). But still, the prophet, even though acting under the inspiration of God's own Spirit, by no means always wins. In the book of Amos there is a protracted discussion between God and his prophet (7.1ff); the prophet turns down several of God's proposals and wins mercy for his people. But at the end God stands firm.

In the New Testament the situation changes, but the view remains the same. Under the new covenant all those who are in Christ are authorised to pray, because all are priests and prophets. We are all baptised into him who is prophet, priest and king; we become a priestly people, who therefore have a right to approach God, and we have all drunk of the prophetic Spirit, who inspires us to speak intimately with God as our Father. But this development must not mislead us into taking prayer for granted. Prayer becomes a duty for us only because it is first an immense privilege. And it is a privilege that never becomes, simply, a right.

But as well as offering a theory and theology of prayer, we can also glean from the Scriptures some very practical directions on the practice of prayer.

1. *Postures for prayer*. There are three common postures for prayer that men and women of faith have adopted. First, *standing* for prayer. It is in this posture that Abraham comes before the Lord to plead for the people of Sodom (Genesis 18.22) and that Hannah chooses to intercede for her son Samuel (I Samuel 1.26). Standing for prayer is the preferred posture of Solomon when he dedicates the Temple in Jerusalem, a home for the ark of the covenant (1 Kings 8.22). Daniel chooses to *kneel* as he prepares to face the lions in their den. 'When Daniel learned that the decree had been published, he went home to his upstairs room where the windows opened towards Jerusalem. Three times a day he got down on his knees and prayed, giving thanks

to his God, just as he had done before' (Daniel 6.10). Finally, *prostration* has been favoured by those with pressing and urgent needs, as with Moses and Aaron (Numbers 16.45) before the wrath of the Lord, as with Elijah on Mount Carmel following the destruction of the prophets of Baal (1 Kings 18.42), and none more poignantly than Jesus in the Garden of Gethsemane (Matthew 26.39) as he struggles to be obedient to the will of the Father that he should embrace the cross. Although some have speculated that King David's prayer (2 Samuel 7.18) in an apparently *sitting* position indicates a fourth posture, this is doubtful. Of course, the position of the body is by no means the only element of posture. The attitude of the lands has a significant place here. These were *lifted* (Psalm 63.4) and *spread out*, with upturned palms symbolic of the act of receiving.

Posture in prayer is important and the Bible offers a variety of possibilities which still have considerable currency. For when we pray, we pray not only with our head or our heart, it is as the Orthodox say, a 'being before God with the head in the heart'. It is an experience of the whole person – body, mind and spirit – and therefore bodily posture is very much part and parcel of the prayer itself, affirming, reflecting the mind and the mood of prayer itself. And this is true as much for personal prayer as it is for public worship. And I have to say that, whilst I am utterly sympathetic to the possibility of a greater freedom of expression in public worship, there is nevertheless a profound sense of the praying community when, in no sense in a regimented kind of way, the whole congregation is seated or standing or, more rarely sadly these days, kneeling.

Physical posture and gesture is an essential ingredient in prayer, as we seek to lay before God the whole of what we do and are. In this regard I think, for example, of that very powerful moment before ordination when candidates and congregation are kneeling silently whilst the lines of the *Venite Creator Spiritus* are intoned. I think of the Veneration of the Cross on Good Friday when the cross is proclaimed before the people with the words, 'This is the wood of the cross', and all bend the knee with the words, 'Oh, come let us worship.' I think of the time, some twenty-five years ago now, when in the oppressive Stalinist-style communist regime of Nicolae Ceausescu, in a crowded tramcar or on a train or just simply walking by a wayside shrine, individuals would make the sign of the cross and close their eyes momentarily in prayer. I think of the small village in the west of Madagascar to which we travelled about three years ago on a very hot day with their new bishop, where drums and dancing – and very fervent dancing it was at that – were the experience of praise and thanksgiving to God. I think, too, of a hand held and a brow stroked at the bedside of a comatose and dying patient – simply an expression of confidence and hope in the God who has created and redeemed and saved us. So posture, gesture, the physical, are vitally important aspects of prayer – aspects which are currently much in vogue as we seek to ensure that we do not lose touch with our bodies, with our very selves, in a world where stress and tension seem to dominate so much of our lives.

2. *Places for prayer*. A survey of preferred places of prayer can reveal insights into the faith and understanding of our forebears. In the Old Testament the books of Samuel and Kings contain the richest material. The ark denoted the local presence of God and therefore the place of prayer. So Hannah (1 Samuel 1) and David (2 Samuel 7) are concerned to come before the Lord in that place. But as sacrifice is offered at 'high places', prayer may be offered there also. Consequently Samuel travels up to Mizpah (1 Samuel 7.5) and Solomon to Gibeon (1 Kings 3). When the temple is dedicated it is as a house of prayer (1 Kings 8), and interestingly Solomon's prayer struggles with the concept of a God who is both present in that particular place and yet whose presence can neither be contained nor limited. In the New Testament, Jesus can be seen to emphasise the importance of finding private places for prayer. This is in order to avoid the temptation of doing anything for the sake of outward show. Jesus often retreats to the mountain in order to be alone, and encourages his disciples not to pray standing in the synagogues

and on the street corners but rather to go into their rooms and close the door (Matthew 6.6). For the early church there was a period of uneasy coexistence with Judaism before the two traditions went their separate ways. To ordinary observers, the Christians were only a new sect of Judaism. They had their private worship (Acts 2.42) but they did not on that account forsake the temple; and it is possible that they still attended the synagogues, though there is no evidence on this point beyond the practice of St Paul on his missionary journeys (in which case he had a special object in view) and James 2.2, although this could refer to a distinctively Christian assembly.

3. *Times for prayer.* St Peter observes the sixth hour (Acts 10.9) and he and St John go up to the temple at the ninth hour, which is described as the hour of prayer (Acts 3.1). It is probable that the gathering described in Acts 2.1 was for worship and this is fixed by 2.15 as having taken place at the third hour, so there is evidence of all three Jewish hours of prayer.

Furthermore, there is no doubt that in the earliest liturgical documents as well as in the patristic writings, the hours of prayer persisted, indeed so persisted that they became embedded ultimately within the monastic tradition – a tradition which is common today. Whilst discussions in such establishments centre around a threefold Office, a fivefold Office, a sevenfold Office or whatever, the aim is the same – the sanctification of time through the structured penetration of the day with prayer appropriate to the time, morning, noon and evening. Indeed such prayers are provided for in the most recent book produced from within our own Anglican tradition entitled *Celebrating Common Prayer: A version of the Daily Office SSF.* And as the Archbishop of Canterbury rightly reminds us in his Foreword,

> Although the Services are conceived for corporate use, they can also be adapted easily so that people may use them when alone. We need to recognize and cater for the many Christians who are not part of a family which shares their

faith. We need to recognize too that there are many occasions when people may have need of a structured form of prayer when they are on their own, whether it is in hospital or on a commuter train, those peculiar forms of isolation when there are many people around us.[4]

And speaking again from my own experience of those 'peculiar forms of isolation when there are no people around', again I recall the time of my ministry in eastern Europe when I was attached to the Theological Institute in Bucharest, and when the recitation of the daily offices of Morning and Evening Prayer, the Psalmody and the Scripture readings became a very powerful support in difficult circumstances – the support of the wider Church praying the same prayers, saying the same psalms, reading the same Scriptures. Times for prayer are important, as has always been recognized by religious people, not least those in the Christian tradition itself.

4. *Patterns for prayer*. If we were now to enquire what models, what examples of prayer the Scriptures set out, the response would necessarily be that all manners and styles of prayer find their place, from Genesis 4.26 – 'Then began people to call upon the Name of the Lord' – to the closing pages of the New Testament in the book of Revelation, where peoples from every tribe and nation and tongue stand before the throne of God in their ceaseless hymn of praise.

There are elements of real exchange and dialogue between God and the individual, with Abraham and with Moses. Intercession is prominent in the prayer of the Patriarchs, and there are a considerable number of personal prayers too – Genesis 15.2, a prayer for a son; Genesis 24.12, Elias on his journey. Jacob's first prayer was a vow (Genesis 28.20), his prayer in Genesis 32.9–12 is in favour of Esau. Patriarchal blessings are prayers. For when one person 'blesses' another it is precisely a vision of the divine purpose for the person blessed, and a declaration of it. It is prophetic; it is also a prayer.

Prayer in the Scriptures, just as in our own experience, changes considerably with circumstances. Thus in the post-exilic period prayer becomes more the nature of confession, both personal and communal. The sin of Israel is acknowledged and God's righteousness and justice are proclaimed and celebrated. Thus, for example, Nehemiah takes upon himself the sins of Israel and confesses them as a whole (1.6). He is an intercessor, but as such does not stand apart from those for whom he intercedes. He is part and parcel of their guilt and of their confession of turning away from God.

Already I have touched upon the Psalms. It has been written of them that they exceed in content and variety all other prayers of the Old Testament – and so they do. However I would just like to add at this point two further aspects with regard to the Psalms. The first is concerned with those which are described as 'cursing' psalms and which at one time were excluded from the Psalter, then appeared with brackets around the offending parts, and still do – omitted by some, used by others. But to omit such verses and such psalms has always seemed to me to miss the point. Our worship may have become very gentile and anodyne, but there is no way in which, when we come before God in prayer, the God unto whom all hearts are open, all desires known, we can evade or avoid the kind of people that we are, or indeed the sort of feelings we may have. It may be fairly straightforward to articulate those deep-down things which are not too much of a course of stumbling or a matter of offence to us and to others. But what of our anger – that blazing furnace within which can so easily erupt and which desperately so often we seek to hide – anger before God, anger against a fellow human being. Those deep-down feelings of hostility too – of lust and hatred – they need to be released and set free, and it is my belief that the Psalter provides exactly the right sort of vehicle whereby in our silence and solitude before the Lord we can dare to speak out in the words of the psalmist what otherwise we should be either embarrassed or ashamed even to think of. We have such an example in our own Anglican Cycle, on the Sixth

Sunday before Christmas, where Psalm 58 is bracketed in the Lectionary and where it is bracketed in its entirety in the Psalter. Now I am not sure just how often ordinary Anglicans pray that God will break in their mouths the teeth of their adversaries that they might wither like trodden grass and that in God's smiting them, we shall rejoice by way of bathing our feet in their blood. Yes, it is all a bit 'over the top', as we might say. Yet we should beware, for every human person has the potential for such intense passion and feeling and most of us have surely experienced it at one time or another. We may not express it in exactly these words – indeed we may express it even more vehemently – but to evade the matter altogether seems to me to be a dangerous omission so far as our prayer is concerned. The Scriptures provide us with a model by which we are given not only permission but also a way in which to handle the intensity of such thoughts and feelings before God.

Closely connected with the use of the Psalms in such an amazing variety of situations and circumstances in our prayer, there emerged fairly early on a collection of Psalter Collects – that is, actual prayers based on the Psalms. I am enormously gratified to find that this same idea now has a place in the new book to which I referred earlier, *Celebrating Common Prayer*, where at the end of each psalm an appropriate prayer is produced. Thus in the case of Psalm 58 to which I have just referred – the following is provided: 'Do not face us, O living God, with the choice of a world without justice or a future without mercy; in your mercy establish justice and in your justice remember your overflowing mercy in Jesus Christ our Lord.'[5]

When we turn to the New Testament there is the personal example of Jesus himself. It is perhaps worth noting at this stage the particular points in Jesus' life when the evangelists note that Jesus prays. First, at or before significant events in his life – at his baptism, before choosing the twelve, before the Transfiguration, to name but a few. There is, of course, the prayer made in Gethsemane, to which I want to return in a few moments.

Secondly, Jesus prays before the performance of miracles.

He also prays for others – the prayer of intercession – and in this regard the extended prayer of John 17 for unity, for his immediate followers as well as those who were to come after, that they may be one that the world might believe, is a very timely prayer for ourselves as a Church.

I want for a moment to return to the prayer in Gethsemane, that prayer of anguish and struggle, which is so deep and so intense and so dark that 'his sweat became like great drops of blood falling down upon him'. In deep distress and trouble Jesus prays, 'If it be possible that this hour might pass from me'; and linked with this, of course, must surely be the cry from the cross, the opening verse of Psalm 22: 'My God, My God, why hast thou forsaken me? Here, surely, is a prayer the like of which many of us have experienced to some degree – the prayer which we make when God seems more absent from us than he is present to us; the prayer of utter helplessness and hopelessness; the prayer not only of desolation but also of disillusion as we experience a deep God-forsakenness, the darkness and blackness of despair about ourselves and God. Here, in Gethsemane, Jesus takes this upon himself in the prayer which he makes before the Father, and at the same time gives us the way and the will ourselves to know the costliness of obedient and self-giving love – 'Not my will, but thine, be done.'

There is also the silence of Jesus, which I believe to be a potent factor – those times when he 'answers them never a word'. And it is a stillness and silence which is present throughout the biblical record – those times and moments and events and circumstances in which all human power fails and when the only real response can be to 'let go and let God'. I think, for example, of the Israelites fleeing from Egypt, pursued by the Egyptian hosts, as they are suddenly confronted by the waters of the Red Sea.' Moses' advice is in Exodus 14.13 (in the course of massive complaints from the people): 'Fear not, stand firm, and see the salvation of the Lord which he will work for you today; for the Egyptians whom you see today you shall never see again. The Lord will fight for you and you have only to be still.' Very risky advice in the circumstances, but the right advice none the less. Often the mysterious work of God is effected in silence and away from the multitude – aside from the crowd. So it was in the mighty act of God's raising Jesus from the dead. There is the pattern, too, of Jesus going up into the mountain, out on to the hillside, in order to reflect and pray. Those who have had the privilege and pleasure of making a journey to the Holy Land and visiting the townships around the Sea of Galilee such as Capernaum will recognise all too well the need for going out to the hillside in order to find the silence and space from the din of the narrow streets. And this aspect of Jesus' own practice has a fundamental place in the tradition and life of the Church. Certainly within our own Anglican framework there is an increasing demand for retreat and spiritual direction and refreshment which almost outstrips the possibility of meeting such a demand at the present time. There is also the related and important aspect of silence in public worship – where care is needed if silence is not to be an unexpected and inappropriate time when the congregation considers that perhaps the vicar has lost his place or his mind, rather than the opportunity afforded for deeper and more personal reflection in the context of the worship of the whole community.

It cannot be without significance that immediately after Christ revealed himself to Paul on the Damascus Road it is said of Paul, 'Behold, he is praying' (Acts 9.11). Probably for the first time Paul discovered what prayer really was, so dramatic and profound was the change effected in him by his conversion. And from that moment Paul proved himself a man of prayer whose dependence on a daily communion with the Lord is evidenced again and again in his letters to the infant churches. The epistles reveal some penetrating insights into the heart and mind of Paul as he continually breaks out into prayer. In Romans 1.8–12 he pours out his heart to God with thanksgiving, intercedes for his friends in Rome and declares that he, too, is depending upon them for support and strength: 'Let me begin by thanking my God, through Jesus Christ, for you all, because the story of your faith is being told all over the world.' In Ephesians 1.15–19 Paul thanks God for the fruits of his ministry in the lives of those who have come to faith in Christ, and prays that they may receive the Spirit through whom comes knowledge of God and illumination of heart. Again, in Ephesians 3.14–18 Paul pleads with the Father for his fellow-Christians: 'With this in mind, then, I kneel in prayer to the Father, from whom every family in heaven and on earth takes its name, that out of the treasures of his glory he may grant you inward strength and power through his Spirit.' In Colossians (1.9f) Paul again prays that the believers should know God's will through spiritual wisdom and understanding, that practice might echo profession and that they might be thankful for their immense privilege and position in the Lord Jesus. Perhaps Paul's greatest contribution to our understanding of Christian prayer is in establishing its connection with the Holy Spirit. Prayer is in fact a gift of the Spirit (1 Corinthians 14.14–16), the believer prays 'in the Spirit' (Ephesians 6.18; Jude 20); so prayer is a co-operation between God and the believer.

So then my theme has been prayer and the Scriptures. If I were to give my own personal testimony, I have to say that one of the most formative periods in my own life in this regard was as a member of a cathedral choir – indeed the very cathedral where, many years later I was first entrusted with episcopal ministry. I still have the Bible which I carried into church with me twice every Sunday for some six or so years. And it is impossible, surely, to sing through the Psalms in this way and to hear the Scriptures regularly read, without their impinging in some degree upon one's consciousness. So there are situations and circumstances in which, almost unconsciously and actually without thinking very much about it, a particular verse of Scripture, a verse or passage from one or other of the psalms, will come to me quite spontaneously. This, I believe, is a gift from God – something to hang on to, something to reflect upon, something to chew over. I can still very well recall the text used throughout the first retreat I ever made – Psalm 46.10: 'Be still, and know that I am God.'

Now I have to confess that I have made no particular effort to remember these things. Unlike my predecessor Bishop Bonner, I have not learned them by heart. What has happened is that the use of the Scriptures in public worship and personal prayer has, I believe, produced this sort of memory bank. And that is why I continue to believe that it is so important that, along with the many other aspects of the Scriptures of which as a bishop I need to be aware, particularly in the preparation of sermons and other matters exegetical and critical, I must also pray the Scriptures and allow them to speak in me and to me; otherwise I shall hear only the rather confused and noisy babblings both of the Church and of the world.

I hope I have been able to share some aspects of the way in which Scripture gives us both examples and models for our prayer. After all, they reflect the experience of those seeking to be faithful to God under the old as well as under the new Covenant – and human nature has not really changed all that much over the years. To ignore such a fund of experience would be irresponsible. Moreover, the Scriptures themselves have been so vital in the development of our Anglican heritage and in the formation of a more distinctive English spirituality. This heritage has produced for us, for example, the *Private Prayers* of Lancelot Andrewes, John Cosin's *Collection of Private Devotions*, Archbishop Laud's *Summary of Devotions*, Jeremy Taylor's *The Rule and Exercises of Holy Living*, John Keble's *The Christian Year*, and so on. How right Archbishop Cranmer was in the first chapter of the first book of his Homilies entitled 'A fruitful exhortation to the reading and knowledge of Holy Scripture', where he writes,

Unto a Christian man, there can be nothing either more necessary or profitable than the knowledge of Holy Scripture; forasmuch as in it is contained God's true word, setting forth his glory and also man's duty. And there is no truth nor doctrine, necessary for our justification and everlasting salvation, but that is or may be drawn out of that fountain and well of truth.

It is this fountain and well of truth which I commend afresh to all of you, which in its own words is truly 'a lantern unto our feet and a light unto our path', both now and for the future, as it has been in the past.

6

THE LITURGICAL USE
OF SCRIPTURE

Philip Goodrich

As parish priest and bishop, I have said the offices of Morning
and Evening Prayer daily throughout the year for thirty-eight
years. No other form of prayer in Christendom can be more
Scriptural than they. They are avenues, if you like, to the great
centrepiece of the Church, namely the Eucharist, itself couched
in Scriptural terms. How could it be otherwise, since the Scriptures record the mighty acts of God and it is those we celebrate
in the Holy Reunion, or the Holy Communion, of the Church?

Let me first give certain pointers to the development of my
subject. The Church preceded the Scriptures of the New Testament. The Scriptures were largely formed to be read at the
occasions of worship of the early Church. Eventually the liturgy
of the Church was steeped in biblical imagery and language, as it
is today. When we consider the liturgical use of the Bible we
consider the Bible as a whole. Of course we need to know about
biblical criticism, form criticism and all the fruits of scholarship
which inform us how the Bible was constructed. It is, however,
important also to see the panorama of the Bible. Reading it
liturgically, day by day and week by week, we move in that
panorama. As a result we are shaped. We see ourselves in a big
setting. We understand who we are and what we could become.
What is more, we join a cavalcade. In that cavalcade which is
God's pilgrim Church on earth, we make for our journey's end.
We are travellers with a dual passport, citizens of earth and
citizens of heaven. The saying of the liturgy and the reading of

the Bible within it cause us to illuminate both earth and heaven. They evoke faith and they strengthen it.

So much for the introduction. Let me now turn to some of those themes.

In Acts 2.42 we read of the first Christians that, 'they met constantly to hear the apostles teach, and to share the common life, to break bread, and to pray.' That infant Church, as we all know, would have only the Old Testament Scriptures to read. However, the oral tradition about Christ obviously became more and more important: 'They met constantly to hear the apostles teach.' As time went on, the number of Christian congregations grew and were spread far and wide. On his travels Paul, the great missionary, dealt with various burning issues and his letters would be read. Similarly, other letters were written by other apostles to deal with specific issues like baptism or controversies raised in the climate of the times.

When the eyewitnesses of Christ's ministry began to die it was necessary to put together in writing collections of his teachings and activities, for the edification of the faithful when they met for worship. St Luke, in the preface to his Gospel, expresses it neatly:

> Many writers have undertaken to draw up an account of the events that have happened among us, following the traditions handed down to us by the original eyewitnesses and servants of the gospel. And so I in my turn, your Excellency, as one who has gone over the whole course of these events in detail, have decided to write a connected narrative for you, so as to give you authentic knowledge about the matters of which you have been informed.

It is probable that the description of the passion of Christ and his resurrection was written separately and read as a separate body of writing. The purpose of this was clearly stated by St John, somewhat later than Mark, Matthew and Luke: 'These things,' he said, 'have been written in order that you may hold the faith that Jesus is the Christ, the Son of God, and that through this faith you may possess life by his name,' (John 20.31).

Jesus' words and deeds were brought together in the form of a simple narrative in order to show the early Church the ground of its faith. The narrative also provided support in the Church's mission, in its preaching, instruction and debate with opponents. The Gospels are missionary writings rather than sophisticated literature. It is clear also from the sermons of the apostles in the book of Acts that much reference back to the Old Testament writings enabled the disciples to see their experience in a large setting, and to see it as a moment of revelation. Upon them had the end of the world come.

It was not until the latter part of the second century that the first official collection of writings, known as the Muratorian Canon was formed. The full canon of the New Testament followed 150 years later. In 367 Athenasius, in a Festal Epistle, gives the list of new Testament writers we now have. An official declaration of the canon had to wait until the Council of Trullo in the seventh century.

I have said that eventually the liturgy of the Church was steeped in biblical language. Look at The Book of Common Prayer: 'We have erred and strayed from thy ways like lost sheep,' recalling Isaiah 53.6, 'All we like sheep have gone astray'. 'That we may evermore dwell in him and he in us' comes from St John chapter 6, as indeed does the whole of the Prayer of Humble Access. The 'Holy, holy, holy' of the Eucharist is from Isaiah chapter 6, and the post-Communion prayer in The Alternative Service Book, 'Father of all, we give you thanks and praise that when we were still far off you met us in your Son and brought us home . . .' has echoes of the story of the Prodigal Son in Luke 15. To add to all this, the canticles, except for the *Te Deum*, are from Scripture, as of course are the Psalms.

The Psalms have been described as the necessary roughage for a Christian diet. Opinions vary about their use. Of course they are unparalleled expressions of worship and paeans of praise. They also express profound penitence and deep longing for God: 'Have mercy upon me, O God, after thy great goodness: according to the multitude of thy mercies do away my offences'

(Psalm 51). 'Like as the hart desireth the water-brooks; so longeth my soul after thee, O God' (Psalm 42). There is a tide running in religion and in the behavioural sciences which encourages us to express our feelings rather than to bottle them up. The exercise is morally neutral, but cathartic. As the body has to get rid of impurities, so also does the soul: 'I will beat them as small as dust before the wind: I will cast them out as the clay in the streets' (Psalm 18.42). 'Wilt not thou slay the wicked, O God: depart from me, ye bloodthirsty men' (Psalm 139.19). 'Let them not say in their hearts, There, there, so would we have it: neither let them say, We have devoured him' (Psalm 35.25). Well, you say these things in the Psalms – you might be thinking about some elements of the tabloid press. Then, when you actually meet them, you can summon the Christian charity which is necessary!

Other people maintain that the enemies which came in for so much rough language in the Psalms are the enemies of our soul, the 'envy, hatred, malice and all uncharitableness', not to mention adulterous thoughts, upon which we must wage continual warfare with a determination to shoot to kill. This also is a valid use of the Psalms. I have a gardener who is very good in many ways and has imaginative ideas for the garden, but I cannot get him to hate weeds! Somehow he does not seem to notice sow thistles, fat hen or groundsel all ready to spread their seeds for another year. 'Yea, I hate them right sore; even as though they were mine own enemies,' (Psalm 139.22). There are also spiritual weeds which need to be pulled up.

Some people speak of the Psalms as borders from which we pluck nosegays along the way. Certainly the Psalms can provide the vocabulary of our prayers. We come before God in silence at the break of the day: 'O God thou art my God: early will I seek thee' (63.1). We are ill or troubled: 'Yea, the darkness is no darkness with thee, but the night is as clear as the day: the darkness and light to thee are both alike' (139.11). We have been let down by friends: 'Yea, even my own familiar friend whom I trusted . . . hath laid great wait for me' (41.9); 'O put not your trust in princes nor in any child of man: for there is no help in them' (146.2). You are about to fly on a fourteen-hour flight or travel a long journey by sea: 'If I take the wings of the morning: and remain in the uttermost parts of the sea; even there also shall thy hand lead me: and thy right hand shall hold me' (139.9–10). And of course there are the moments of affirmation: 'O put thy trust in God: for I will yet give him thanks, who is the help of my countenance and my God' (42.15).

That the Psalms have been used by countless other Christians on their spiritual journey is the source of their strength to us – 'these are words you may trust.'

I have said that when we enact the liturgy and read the words of Scripture we do so as those entering into a cavalcade. We borrow the light of other pilgrims. We could even say that God allows us to put on their faith; so that I might borrow the courage of Terry Waite, or the generosity of Bishop Edward King, even the joy of Francis of Assisi, or the steadfastness of countless unknown Christian people of every century.

Charles Williams has described heaven as a party where every guest wore a costume made from the virtues of other people:

> This guest his brother's courage wore;
> that, his wife's zeal, while, just before,
> she in his steady patience shone;
> there a young lover had put on
> the fine integrity of sense
> his mistress used; magnificence
> a father borrowed of his son,
> who was not there ashamed to don
> his father's wise economy.
> No he or she was he or she
> merely.[1]

Of course, in this heaven there is but one glory. It is the glory of Christ himself in his followers.

To return to the Psalms, known by Christ and used by him: when we use them he is praying in us, his body, the Church.

We are going on with Christ. I remember a friend of mine going to Bishopthorpe when Cyril Garbett was Archbishop of York. Garbett was in his eighties. My friend said he would never forget seeing and hearing the determined old man saying the Psalms purposefully, 'Going on with Christ' to the end which is no end.

Whatever other purpose psalms may have, they are for reflection. At one time the verse would be read or sung by a lector or a cantor, so that the rest could meditate upon it. They would then say or sing a response every third or fourth verse. Suffice it to say that the psalmist is not a religious genius who propounds answers. Rather, he is an ordinary person of faith who sometimes expressed profound misgivings: 'Then thought I to understand this, but it was too hard for me, until I went into the house of God' (73.15–16). Eventually he says, 'It is good for me that I have been in trouble, for thereby I learn thy statutes' (119.71).

There is, of course, a place for the expression of despair, even an owning of it, in order to see that God has some better purpose for us: 'Man being in honour hath no understanding: but is compared unto the beasts that perish' (49.20) 'He shall follow the generation of his fathers and never see light' (49.19) Very despairing! Yet the next Psalm, 50, begins with the affirmation, 'The Lord, even the most mighty God has spoken: and called the world from the rising up of the sun unto the going down thereof.'

Perhaps it was from the Psalms that Blake found inspiration for his well-known verse:

> Man was made for Joy and Woe;
> And when this we rightly know,
> Thro' the World we safely go,
> Joy and woe are woven fine
> A clothing for the soul divine.[2]

I have said that the liturgical use of the Bible suspends for the occasion our critical concern. This does not mean that we suddenly become fundamentalists or obscurantists. It means that we certainly read commentaries, know about the structure of the Pentateuch or the Prophets, and are *au fait* with the formation of the Gospels. We know why there are four Gospels and not one. We know the difference between the Marcan account of the crucifixion and the one in John. We know that the Epistles to Timothy and Titus are written by a different hand from those to the Thessalonians or the Galatians. Nevertheless, for liturgical use, we see the Bible as a whole. The Malvern Hills, the Avon Vale and Bredon Hill are all geologically differently constructed, yet for the purposes of an exhilarating walk this does not matter.

Let it be said that far more use of commentaries should be made in the preparation of sermons. I have no doubt that 'dividing the Word' feeds the faithful as much as does breaking the bread. What I am saying is that those who speak of the liturgical use of Scripture do their critical study in another room.

So let us look at the Bible as a whole. But first a digression. This course of lectures at St Giles-in-the-Fields attracted nearly 700 people, whereas previous courses have had as many as 230 members. The rector, Gordon Taylor, suggested that it may be because people generally feel that the Bible belongs to them. Doctrine and moral theology are the preserve of experts, people with a theological degree, but the Bible belongs to everybody. This is an attractive argument. Ever since the translations into the vulgar tongue by people like Coverdale and Wycliffe, people have stood by the concept of the open Bible. This may have raised as many problems as it has solved, but it has remained a valued freedom in the British Isles for five hundred years. It enabled the British to be described as 'the people of a book and that book the Bible'. Even those who are cast away on the BBC's desert island are allowed a copy of the Bible.

When I was a schoolboy we were living through the dark days of the war. The church bells were silent because they were to be used to announce the invasion of Hitler if it happened. In The Book of Common Prayer the rubric states that the clergyman who ministers in the parish shall, 'cause a bell to be tolled . . . that the people may come to hear God's Word and to pray with him'. It has always occurred to me that the bell for Morning and Evening Prayer announces in a similar way the 'invasion' of our world by the living God, to win us back to his allegiance and thereby to redeem our situation and open for us the gate of glory. It is a simple little analogy, and like all analogies is limited. God, after all, in the incarnation is coming to home territory. 'He was in the world and the world was made by Him.'

Nevertheless, when through the daily and Sunday-by-Sunday liturgy we enter the strange world of the Bible, we enter a world of God's dealings. It is a world where God, not humanity, is the main actor on the stage. It is a story of what God has done for us and for our salvation through the miracle of Bethlehem, the judgement of Calvary and the triumph of the empty grave. The drama enacted is not one of moral progress, though that is involved. It is a drama of redemption. The God who in Old Testament history triumphed gloriously, has done so yet again. Salvation is achieved by divine descent, by God's grace in becoming man. It is not achieved by human ascent, by humanity's attempt to become like God. The Bible is about a deed done by God, a saving act, not a set of propositions or a piece of good advice. We miss the point of the Bible unless we see in it the record of histories, personalities and events through which God is working out his purpose. There is a dynamism about the Bible which shows God, through historical events, moving his people and his world towards that great divine event towards which the whole creation moves, when all things shall bless their creator and 'worship him in humbleness'.

> The God of Abraham praise,
> At whose supreme command
> From earth we rise, and seek the joys
>   At his right hand:
> We all on earth forsake,
> Its wisdom, fame and power;
> And him our only portion make,
>   Our shield and tower.[3]

The analogy of a drama is not a bad one. In the first eleven chapters of Genesis we have the overture to the main work. We see humankind as disobedient, murderous, sensuous and vain. There is judgement and also there is mercy. Then the first act begins. We ring up the curtain to see how things are, lived out on the stage of a nation's history. God's people are called by God to co-operate with him in his grand design for the world. It is a high calling, and the People of God fail to live up to it. The prophets act as a Greek chorus, commenting on the story and drawing out the tragedy: 'Ah, sinful nation. The ox knoweth his owner and the ass his master's crib but Israel does not know. Israel does not understand' (Isaiah 1.3).

Gradually, as each in turn plays a part and retires to the wings, the drama begins to point forward. One person must be raised up to do what the nation had failed to do. He will be a righteous servant in whom God will delight, and he will bear the sins of many.

The first act ends. The curtain rises on the second act with a sense of expectation and true wonder. The centre of the stage is empty. Who will fill it? It is filled, to the astonishment of all, by a helpless child in a manger. As Archbishop Anselm said; 'It hath not pleased the Almighty to save mankind by an argument.' Rather, the vulnerable child stops the show and calls forth our affection and our loyalty.

> Welcome, all wonders in one sight!
> Eternity shut in a span.
> Summer in winter. Day in night.
> Heaven in earth and God in man.
> Great little one! whose all-embracing birth
> Lifts earth to heaven, stoops heaven to earth.[4]

So if Act One of the drama is about the story of a nation, Act Two is about the story of a person, unfolded in the Gospels. It seems to end in failure as the hero dies between two thieves on a cross outside the city where he should have been enthroned. What then is left for the third act?

Yet again there is surprise. That which seemed like an end was in fact a beginning. The third act involves audience participation, and people are still taking part, still taking sides, prompted and produced by the Holy Spirit of God who makes us strong to play our part. The drama is a universal one and played out on the world's stage. It is important that we should not miss our cue or muff our lines. How Act Three will end no one knows, not even the angels of God. It is in the hands of the Author of it all, and he is the God of surprises.

Forgive my analogy. It is one to think about. The fact is that when we use the liturgy, either at the Parish Communion or in the daily offices of Morning and Evening Prayer, we enter the panorama of the Bible. We enact the liturgy. We do not just read it. In that strange world we discover who we are and what we could become. It is a world which shapes us and makes us.

Luckily we have improved our lectionary. We should not be too selective nor too thematic. We should let the Bible speak for itself. In *Celebrating Common Prayer*, the new Franciscan Prayer Book,[5] it is suggested that when small groups meet for worship they should have the Bible on a stand as a focal point of their worship. To a certain extent, if we climb Everest because it is there, we should read the Bible because it is there, love songs of the Song of Songs and all. More and more we shall gain insights into the ways of God with humankind. We shall not always immediately see the relevance, nor understand every line. Some readings from the Bible will have the quality of verbal sculpture and will be to us a symbol, like the reading of the opening chapter of St John's Gospel at Christmas. We do not fully understand, but the words resonate within us and speak of incarnation and Christmas.

Much biblical imagery and language is evocative. In the liturgy it would be wrong to dissolve the evocation by critical analysis. 'Behold, a virgin shall conceive and bear a son, and shall call his name Immanuel (Isaiah 7.14). Think of other titles for Jesus drawn from tradition, well said by others and now apt for a new meaning – Key of David, Desire of all nations, Redeemer, Saviour, Lord.

To move in the world of God's dealings gives us a new viewpoint and opens up exciting possibilities for ourselves and our world. It does this in a robust, unselfconscious way. The best influence is the one which is unselfconscious in both the giver and the receiver. When you read the Bible liturgically you do not have to stop and say, 'Now there's a moral in this little tale.' There may be, but more important than that is that God is in it and we also are involved. We learn to see that God is in the world of every day upon which the Bible stories shed their light.

Baron von Hügel, the Roman Catholic lay theologian whose work became widely read in the 1920s and 1930s, said in his book on Catherine of Genoa that if Christianity is to be a universal faith, it must have three elements – the institutional, the intellectual and the evangelical. The institutional element is the means by which the riches of Christ are conveyed to us through liturgy, credal formularies, art, architecture, music, literature, custom and chivalry. There is a whole storehouse of joy which we call Christian civilisation, and Christ in His fullness and majesty can be conveyed through these things, otherwise how could he be conveyed through sacraments at all?

The intellectual element is, of course, essential to Christian life. It is the intellectual rigour which unpacks the tradition of its meaning to each new generation and adds to it and enhances it. The evangelical element, not using that word in a party label sense, is the personal commitment of the individual who has found something in Christ without which life is a diminished thing. 'Oh taste and see how gracious the Lord is!' Of course, these elements, the intellectual and the evangelical, are integral.

However, we have to remember that the white light which is Christ is so bright and dazzling that we sometimes have to look at it as it is mirrored in the reflecting surfaces of the culture of succeeding centuries. Many many people can only comprehend Christ and receive his riches in this way. It is rather a Platonic theory, but it is sometimes a relief to many who cannot answer the question, 'Have you given yourself to Jesus? Do you know him?' Such escapees from aggressive evangelism are relieved to encounter the living God through liturgy and the liturgical use of Scripture. We should add, of course, that the woman who touched the hem of Christ's garment eventually had to turn, face him, and answer his questions.

So the liturgical use of the Bible enables us to be changed while remaining robustly ourselves for the encounters of the real world of business, commerce and the knockabout of every day. We do not become so heavenly-minded as to be no earthly use. 'In the presence of God, I beseech you, be there in your own character, nor fear lest any come more worthy than yourself.' I cannot remember who said that, but it is a very Anglican sentiment and an appropriate sentiment for a Church which is not a sect nor a gathered Church, but the English nation at prayer!

So often, in the 1960s and 1970s, when I was a parish priest, my sermons were about the Church's need to change, or the stewardship of money, or the rightness of ordaining women. A churchwarden, who was a knight of the shires and member of Parliament, frequently told me of his preference for the great stories of the Old Testament – Naboth's vineyard, David and Goliath, Elijah and the prophets of Baal. To hear the words, 'How long halt ye between two opinions? If God be God, serve him' (1 Kings 18.21), was to tone up for the many decisions of every day. The Bible is the people's book.

There is a delightful passage in Thomas Hardy's *Far from the Madding Crowd*. It is a discussion in a pub in which a character called Coggan speaks of being a staunch Church of England man:

'I've never changed a single doctrine: I've stuck like plaster to the old faith I was born in. Yes, there's this to be said for the church, a man can belong to the church and bide in his own cheerful old inn, and never trouble or worry his mind about doctrines at all. But to be a meetinger, you must go to chapel in all winds and weathers, and make yourself as frantic as a skit. Not but that chapel-members be clever chaps enough in their way. They can lift up beautiful prayers out of their own heads, all about their families and shipwrecks in the newspaper.'

'They can, they can', said Mr Clark, with corroborative feeling, 'but we churchmen, you see, must have it all printed aforehand, or dang it all, we should no more know what to say to a great gaffer like the Lord than babes unborn.'[6]

The two speakers then become more defensive and feel inadequate towards meetingers with their extempore prayers. Is their inadequacy not misplaced? To 'have it all printed aforehand' is not a sign of spiritual inadequacy but a chosen way of sharing the riches of the People of God of all times and all places. The Jewish people were notably good at talking about God. If it has been well said by them, why not draw on their wealth? We all need resonances and stirrings of our unconscious as out of the Bible deep calls to deep. We read – no, we rehearse – those events which brought our faith to birth. They remind us that God is as he is, and that worship is in order. A critical approach to the text is not rejected. It is suspended. When you go in to bat you do not take a copy of the rules of cricket to read at the end of every over. So on great national occasions it is possible to thrill to the words of 'Zadok the priest and Nathan the prophet' without going too deeply into the origins of the text. The same Spirit of God who transfigured the occasion of Solomon's coronation has power to transfigure the events of our contemporary world and evoke and strengthen faith.

The Book of Common Prayer shall have nearly the last word. 'For they so ordered the matter that all the whole Bible . . . should be read over once every year . . . that the people (by daily hearing of holy Scripture read in the Church) might continually profit more and more in the knowledge of God, and be the more inflamed with the love of his true religion.' Over three hundred years later the Preface to The Alternative Service Book adds these vital words:

> But words, even agreed words, are only the beginning of worship. Those who use them do well to recognise their transience and imperfection; to treat them as a ladder, not a goal; to acknowledge their power in shaping faith and kindling devotion, without claiming they are fully adequate to the task.[7]

7

PREACHING
FROM A TEXT
Hugh Montefiore

Since this is not a sermon, it doesn't strictly speaking need a text. I thought of a verse from Proverbs: 'Pleasant words are as an honeycomb, sweet to the soul, and health to the bones' (16.24). But a text is not always properly described as 'pleasant': it may be acerbic. Slightly more apt would be another of the proverbs of Solomon: 'A word fitly spoken is like apples of gold in pictures of silver' (25.11). But that describes what a sermon should be rather than its text. I think what best sums up what I have to say is a verse from Hebrews: 'The word of God is quick, and powerful, and sharper than any two-edged sword, piercing even to the dividing asunder of the joints and marrow' (Hebrews 4.12).

It is not always appropriate to preach from a text. It depends partly on the occasion. A sermon at a funeral, an informal address, a eucharistic homily, all may well be delivered without a text. The one absolute rule about sermons is that there are no rules at all, except knowing how to begin and, above all, when to end. In any case, one person's preaching style is very different from another's. None the less, on most occasions I strongly advocate preaching from a text.

I find it a good discipline. It means that we have to take trouble and think out beforehand what we want to say; at the very least thinking out our text, and also, please God, how we intend to apply it. It gives us a framework within which to preach, which is a boon to the preacher and an even greater boon to the congregation. There are other benefits for the congregation as well. We preachers have to face the fact that, though our voice may be as sweet as St Chrysostom the golden-mouthed, and our rhetoric as powerful as St Peter's on the Day of Pentecost, our congregation is not going to remember what we have said (especially if they have to listen to us Sunday after Sunday), any more than they will remember what they have had for Sunday lunch. *But they may well remember the text.* And that brings me to another point. Whenever possible, I choose a text from the Authorised Version, because it is so memorable.

For example, in St John's Gospel, before the resuscitation of Lazareth, Martha exclaims, according to the rather prosaic Jerusalem Bible: 'By this time he will smell', while in the Revised Standard Version we have the refined, 'Lord, by this time there will be an odour.' The robust Authorised Version has, 'Lord, by this time he stinketh' – and surely there can be no doubt which of the three is the most memorable. If, however, the sermon is based on the text from one of the Lessons used during the service, it is better to take the text from the same version – which means finding out beforehand which version is being used. Otherwise there will always be some alert person in the congregation – or there ought to be – who will notice that the preacher's text is worded quite differently from the one that he or she has just heard from the lectern; and the preacher, too, is likely to be somewhat at sea.

The use of a text for a sermon can very greatly increase its impact, especially if it is repeated during the sermon, and particularly at the end. I consider that this is most important at the Eucharist – and in so many churches today this is the only service that is attended by the People of God as a whole. In this case the text will usually be taken from one of the three Lections for the day, and so it will be particularly relevant. There is an exception to this, and that is those Anglican churches which insist on using the Roman Catholic Sunday lectionary, which is no doubt excellent, but it is different from ours. When, as a diocesan bishop, I was visiting such churches I used to persevere in choosing my text from the Anglican readings, if necessary prefacing it by saying, 'As you would have heard if you had used the Anglican lectionary prescribed by law . . .'

The preacher can often learn something from the choice of readings in the Lectionary. For example, in a church where I was preaching one Whitsunday, the vicar told me that he had chosen as the Old Testament option the thunder and lightning at the giving of the Law on Mount Sinai, rather than the alternative reading for Pentecost, the story of Babel with its confusion of tongues. When I asked him why he had done this, he said: 'Oh, I just happen to like the story.' But in fact the reason why this lesson is one of the options is that the Jews kept Pentecost as the Giving of the Law, which was fulfilled in the New Testament by the giving of the Spirit. I was able to choose a text which brought out this illuminating truth.

Choosing a text from the lectionary does not mean that we have to preach the same sermon every two years when the lectionary cycle recurs. In any case, we may well choose some other text from the readings. What I am trying to point out is that not every sermon is of the expository kind, requiring a repetition of the exposition that was given two years earlier. I don't want to decry the expository type of sermon, because I am sure that it has a place; but we have to face the fact that, if we intend to expound a passage as a whole it is not easy for the congregation to follow unless they have in their hands a version of the text, whether in a Bible or in a prayer book. In any case, pure exposition is not much use to people who live nearly two thousand years after the text was composed: it has to be made relevant to their situation. It is probably for this reason that not many sermons today could be described as expository. What people need from the Bible is hermeneutics – that is to say, interpretation for today. What preachers often do is speak aloud their reflections which have been kindled by the text which they have chosen. This is perfectly proper, providing that these reflections are made in an atmosphere of prayer and devotion.

Let us imagine that in this spirit we are reading through the Lessons for next Sunday's Eucharist. Some particular phrase or sentence strikes us. We feel that we can use it as the text of what we will want to say. We meditate on it, and all sorts of images and ideas flow into our mind. We collect our thoughts and order them into ideas and images; and a sermon starts to take shape, with a particular form and a particular message. We rightly use the text at the beginning, and it will be apparent that our reflections flow out of our text, even though in no sense are they an exposition of the text. That is entirely proper, and because our imagination has been stirred by our meditation on this Word of the Lord, it is our hope and expectation that we may stimulate the same process of thought in at least some members of our congregation.

But if we are using the text in a very different sense from that which the author intended, then we are under an obligation to tell the congregation, in the course of what we have to say, the straight meaning of the text as well as the way in which we are using it. As a matter of fact, we can never quite understand the New Testament text (and much less the Old Testament) in exactly the same way as the original author, because he lived in the first century and we live in the twentieth, and so our presuppositions are different; and the English words we use for the text carry different connotations from the Greek in which they were originally written. But if we do not understand them in exactly the same way, we can at least approximate to what the author intended, and we have an obligation to do that.

Perhaps here I should give some illustrations of the point I am making. It is always easier to take examples from one's own experience, and it so happens that in 1991 I had to prepare a course of sermons on the Environment in preparation for the Rio Earth Summit; they were subsequently published under the title *Preaching for our Planet*.[1] Far and away the most enjoyable part of the composition was finding the right text for each of the twenty-two sermons. It meant searching through one's Bible, pursuing a theme; it meant poring over the concordance; it meant looking up books about the Bible, and from time to time looking at the original language of the text. I found it thrilling and invigorating, and I suppose that is why I chose this subject on which to speak. I commend the practice to other preachers. For example, when I was talking about the need for conservation, I had to deal with the teaching of Jesus in the Sermon on the Mount, in particular when he tells us, in the words of the Authorised Version to 'take no thought for the morrow'. This seems at first sight in direct contradiction to the conservationists, who are always telling us to take thought for the future. In fact, when one looks up the original Greek, one finds that the phrase means 'Do not get anxious about . . .', which is quite different, because anxiety always clouds one's judgement. When one has chosen one's text, it is wise to look it up in a Greek New Testament, and (if one can use it) in a Hebrew Bible, because one can often get new light on it in this way.

If we are in the habit of using a text, we find that some will fall naturally into place. For example, when thinking about global warming, I immediately thought of Psalm 19.4–5: 'In them hath he set a tabernacle for the sun, which is as a bridegroom coming out of his chamber'. This started me off on a cheerful note, reminding me of all the blessings of the sun without which we could not be alive. Again, when thinking of water, it was not very difficult to call to mind a text from Psalm 104, with its evocation of the graciousness of God in sending springs into the valleys, to give drink to every beast of the field, and with its mention of the 'great and wide sea in which are things creeping innumerable'. Once again this allowed me to start positively, before going on to see the way in which humankind has abused this resource. I always choose a positive text if I can. When preaching about agriculture, my mind went to Deuteronomy 8, where we are told that 'the Lord thy God brought thee into a good land, a land of brooks of water, of fountains and depths that spring out of valleys and hills, a land of wheat and barley, and vines and fig-trees.' Once again that sort of text can start the sermon off positively before getting on what is actually happening in agriculture today. These are practical examples of how the use of texts can add point to what one is saying, not least because the Bible always puts things in the context of the graciousness or judgement of God. If we look hard enough we can find a text for any sermon we may feel called upon to preach on any subject. It may not actually be on the subject itself, but on the moral or spiritual point we are sharing with our congregation.

But there are also texts of a more forbidding nature. When it came to nuclear power, I thought of 2 Peter 3.10, where there is a prophecy of the Day of the Lord coming as a thief in the night, in which 'the heavens shall pass away with a great noise, and the elements shall melt with fervent heat', and the earth and its works will be burned up. This is an example of a text for which the original meaning must be given; for it is an apocalyptic prophecy with apocalyptic imagery, and one needs to explain that it is not a direct prophecy of what might happen; and one further needs to make it clear that the final 'Day of the Lord' in those days could refer to current events, such as the Fall of Jerusalem, and so it can properly be used in our own time for a nuclear holocaust. A text must never be used in a misleading way: otherwise it can give an unintended impression of fundamentalism. But the use of a text gives added authority to what we say, because we are using the Word of God.

A sermon on acid rain set me something of a problem, until I read that the explosion which destroyed the Cities of the Plain (Genesis 19) would have released gases like hydrogen sulphide, leading to the ignition of asphalt and petroleum; and the sulphur in the atmosphere would certainly have descended in the form of acid rain. Here again the text needed interpretation, for according to Genesis the explosion was the result of the wickedness of Sodom and Gomorrah, whatever that wickedness may have been, while the cause of acid rain today is our thoughtlessness and greedy use of precious resources. This leads me to emphasise again a vital point. When we have chosen our text, we should look it up in a commentary, even if it is only the one-volume commentary on the Bible which I presume all preachers possess, and which every interested lay person ought to possess. I gained the information about hydrogen sulphide and the explosion which destroyed the Cities of the Plain from von Rad's commentary on Genesis[2]. It is very sad how seldom Bible commentaries are in fact used in sermon preparation. They constitute a splendid resource, which is largely unused.

Again, I used my commentary when I came to preach about the thinning of the ozone layer, which now apparently extends over towns in both the northern and southern hemispheres. I read through the book of Revelation until I came to the fourth plague, when men were 'scorched with great heat' (16.9). It was good to read through Revelation as a whole; but here again, when using the text it was necessary to point out that we must not look for literal fulfilment of apocalyptic imagery. As St John sat in that lovely cave on the island of Patmos – if that is where the Apocalypse was written – he certainly did not have in mind the thinning of the ozone layer as he wrote: his mind was brimming with biblical imagery which he used to great effect. (I am sorry if I am saturating you with these ecological texts, but I am using them to illustrate my points.)

How does one preach on a text if one is going to talk about the motor car? Not even Ezekiel, with his vision of the whirring wheels, had ever thought of motor cars. I chose that text where the watchman says that the driving is 'like the driving of Jehu the son of Nimshi, for he driveth furiously' (2 Kings 9.20). Here again, one has to explain the difference between a political rebel driving a one-horse-power chariot and a contemporary road hog putting his foot down in a 2500 cc. gas-guzzling monster; but the connection can be made.

More difficult perhaps is a text for a sermon on a theme such as economics. Yet if we look hard enough we can find biblical guidelines. For example in Proverbs 11.1 we read: 'A false balance is an abomination to the Lord; but a just weight is his delight' – and of course classical economics with its free market does give us a false balance, because it does not take into account the damage done by pollution or the over-use of resources which has to be paid for later. Surely the point that the preacher is trying to make can be strengthened by the use of Scripture as a text in this way! Again, recycling is not a theme which appears directly in the Scriptures, but Jesus does tell the parable of the younger son who wasted his substance with riotous living, which is a pretty good description of what is happening today in the developed world. The use of such a text immediately puts the listeners into the context of God and the teaching of Jesus.

I have taken as examples texts for contemporary subjects, because we may need particular help on these issues. But if we are interpreting the Bible as a whole, or speaking on one of its themes, such as love, or grace, or faith, many texts lie ready to hand. It is when we take a non-biblical subject, and apply to it the teaching of the Scriptures, that we need most help.

You may have noticed that a lot of these texts I have cited come from the Old Testament. In the old days, when people used to come in large numbers to Matins or Evensong, they could be sure of hearing the Old Testament read in church. But nowadays, since the spread of the Parish Communion movement, most people do not attend any other service than the Eucharist; and although The Alternative Service Book provides an Old Testament reading each week in the Eucharistic lectionary, most churches prefer to save time by omitting it, and only very occasionally do they use it instead of the New Testament reading. Since home Bible reading is rare, most people simply neither hear nor know their Old Testament. This particularly applies to young people, since in Religious Education nowadays most teachers prefer to focus on contemporary issues, and there is little direct teaching on the Old Testament. This is a pity, as it is a wonderful treasure house of divine revelation, religious history and religious wisdom, to say nothing of the exquisite language of the Authorised Version. Just because the Jewish religion was concerned with the whole of life, while the interests of the infant church tended to be more church-centred, the Old Testament contains many passages which produce splendid texts for dealing with contemporary issues which ought to form the subject of sermons – though the texts need to be explained within their contexts, and their relevance to contemporary issues needs to be unfolded, and always with a reference to the New Testament included. None the less I realise that most preachers' texts very properly will usually come from the New Testament.

I am aware that my remarks so far need a theology of biblical revelation to undergird them. There are differing views about this. Some people think that every verse in the Bible is directly and verbally inspired by God. In that case the use of the text is obvious, since it consists of the actual Word of God. Since very intelligent people have been known to hold this view, enormously ingenious interpretations have been given to exceedingly unpromising texts. These usually involve interpreting the text in some way other than its literal meaning, which is hardly what verbal inspiration means. I do not propose to argue against such a view. I will content myself with simply saying two things. I do not hold it myself, and I do not believe that it is even a biblical view!

At the other extreme there is the view that the Bible is a sacred book because it deals with sacred subjects, and because it is the only volume to contain early reliable information about Jesus and the primitive Church; but that there is nothing particularly inspired about the Bible as such, it is a book which is at times inspiring rather than inspired. In this case a preacher will often sermonise without the use of a text; or if a text is used, it is not because it is intrinsically valuable, but because it suits the preacher to use it. A particular sentence or phrase may seem particularly felicitous; or it may sum up something which the preacher regards as important, or it may contain information which Christians ought to know and think about.

I do not myself hold either of these extreme positions. I have already explained that I am not a fundamentalist. Neither am I one of those people who regard the Bible as mere religious literature. The Bible contains the Word of God. That is not to say that every word is the Word of God, as though it has been dictated by the Holy Spirit in the same kind of way as Mohammed believed that the Qur'an was handed down word for word from heaven. But it contains the Word of God inasmuch as God can still speak to us with spiritual authority through the writings of Scripture as a whole.

Of course, the biblical writers were affected by the cultural conditions of their time; and of course, being human beings, they got some things wrong. None the less the Bible is a collection of books on which the Church has set its seal of authority. It was made by a people whom God had specially chosen for his self-revelation; and that applies both to the Old and to the New Testament. We cannot understand God's self-revelation without the Bible, and we cannot appreciate it without listening to the deep religious insights and truth that the Bible contains, as well as to the sacred stories contained within it. We cannot appreciate the ministry and teaching of Jesus without the Gospels; and we cannot understand their significance unless we read them through the writings of those who stood near enough to the events to write with insight and authority about them. Since we cannot see Jesus face to face, it is through the written Gospels that we come to know him as God's image, God's wisdom and God's Son. We cannot appreciate the nature and work of the Church without reflecting on the surviving correspondence of the primitive Church, and without meditating on its early history and its imaginative writings such as the book of Revelation.

We are right to use our critical faculties in order to understand the nature of the biblical writings, the sources that they used and the nuances that they contain; and in order to identify any errors and to distinguish cultural relativism from eternal truth. We can then appreciate the Scriptures better, in rather the same way as those who love a piece of music can appreciate it better if they analyse the craftsmanship with which it was composed, the reminiscences of earlier music which it may contain, and the point and counterpoint which is embodied within it. But we love the piece of music as a whole; and all biblical criticism should be devoted to enabling us to appreciate Scripture better as a whole. The Scriptures, or at least each book in the Scriptures, must be appreciated holistically, despite the higher and lower criticisms that are applied to details of the text. These books are inspired as a whole to mediate to us God's holy word.

However, we cannot deal with the Bible as a whole in a sermon, nor even with one of its books. The most we can undertake to do is to explain a biblical passage, or perhaps illustrate some contemporary issue by means of scriptural truth. Since a sermon is more likely to be remembered (and acted upon) if it contains not more than two or at most three striking points, the passage chosen must be short if it is to be effectively used. A sermon is more like a picture than a book; a picture which is painted in vivid colours, and contains two or three memorable objects sketched in in the foreground, with plenty of material more vaguely delineated as background. And when it comes to those foreground features, nothing can encapsulate them better than a text, for reasons which I outlined earlier.

A text takes us back to divine self-revelation: even if it is simply an aphorism from the book of Proverbs, it will have a particular slant, and that slant will be that it is God-centred. A text may not be directly focused on the point that we most want to make; but it will embody some divinely revealed principle or fact or insight that will illuminate that point. A text is memorable, whereas our sermon will probably not be. A text will remind the hearer, probably unconsciously, that our whole Christian faith is focused on the self-revelation of God which forms the subject matter of the Bible. For if the preacher is using a text from the Scriptures, the congregation appreciates that even if the preacher is not using it in the sense intended by the biblical author, he or she intends what is said to be in accordance with the Word of God which is found in the Bible as a whole. And that I regard as of the utmost importance.

Sometimes preachers are at a loss for a subject to preach on. Three sermons a Sunday, if not for fifty-two weeks a year, at least for not less than forty-five, means 135 sermons a year; and since the Church Commissioners require thirty-nine years of service before they will grant a full pension, that means, if my mathematics are correct, some 5,265 sermons, not to mention any weekday addresses. Fortunately for the congregations, these sermons will not all be preached to the same people; but unfortunately for the preacher, they will all be delivered by the same person. It is hardly surprising that enthusiasm may sometimes wane a little, or that inspiration from time to time may seem to dry up! Indeed, we may even ask ourselves as late as Friday, 'What on earth am I going to preach about next Sunday?'

It might perhaps have been better had we thought 'What in heaven am I going to preach about on Sunday?' Be that as it may, one has only to look in one's Bible to find a multitude of enticing texts. First, of course, we will look at the passages set in the Lectionary; but if we find no inspiration there, we can roam wider afield. Have you ever heard a sermon preached from a text in the Apocrypha? Remember that for the majority of the Christian Church, the books of the Apocrypha form an integral part of the Bible as a whole. I have found some ravishing texts from the Wisdom of Solomon, one of which I used when preaching to a boys' school, and another in my series on ecology. Is it perhaps an expository sermon we will preach? Think of all those texts from the Epistle to the Romans crying out for exposition. Is it a hortatory sermon? Think of the multitude of texts from the second half of the Epistles, where St Paul begins 'Wherefore . . .' and then starts on Christian ethics. Of course these need to be applied to the situation today, but that is what preaching is about. Or is it a meditative sermon? Think of those texts in the Fourth Gospel, or the vivid imagery of the book of Revelation. Is it a sermon on the imitation of Jesus? The Gospels are littered with appropriate texts. Is it a sermon on the saints? 'Time would fail me,' wrote the author of the Epistle to the Hebrews, 'to tell of Gideon and of Barak.' Well, when did you last hear a sermon about Gideon and Barak? When did you last hear even a sermon on Moses the friend of God?

There is no better way to lift a preacher's spirits in planning a sermon than to finger through the chapters of the Bible, and to cast our eyes over the hundreds and hundreds of ravishing texts that we will find there.

I realise that what I have been saying is a glimpse of the obvious; but, alas, the obvious is often unsaid. I end with a further, very obvious, thought. A sermon is clearly something very subjective. It reveals the preacher's deepest thoughts and feelings; it uncovers the secrets of our heart as we bare our inmost convictions to the view of the congregation. That is as it should be. I have heard sermonising described as 'character in action'. We must not hide our own convictions if we are to be of help to those who hear us. But on the other hand, the gospel that we preach is not a subjective gospel. It is about something that actually happened on the stage of history. It does not depend for its truth on our feelings or our convictions. The gospel needs to be subjectively appropriated, but it is objectively true. And nothing can better underline this objectivity, in contrast to the subjectivity of the preacher, than to anchor an address on a biblical text.

8

A VARIETY OF VERSIONS:
ISSUES IN PUBLIC WORSHIP
AND PRIVATE STUDY
John Oliver

'They lie in the hell like sheep, death gnaweth upon them, and
the righteous shall have domination over them in the morning:
their beauty shall consume in the sepulchre out of their
dwelling' (Psalm 49.14).

'When the company of the spear-men, and multitude of the
mighty are scattered abroad among the beasts of the people, so
that they humbly bring pieces of silver: and when he hath scattered the people that delight in war; then shall the princes come
out of Egypt' (Psalm 68.30–31).

Yes, well; so there is some reason for new translations. Admittedly these are two of the most obscure verses in the Old Testament, and admittedly they are from the Coverdale translation of
the Psalter. It is also true that the Hebrew text in these cases is
obscure, so that not even modern translators have been able to
make very much sense of them. But they are a reminder to us of
some of the strange obscurities with which people have lived in
the past, before the advent of modern translations, or translations
which have managed to make some kind of coherent sense out
of a difficult text.

I was brought up in my childhood to go fairly regularly to
church, usually to Matins or Evensong. They were, of course,
services from The Book of Common Prayer and the lessons
were always read from the Authorised Version of the Bible. This

meant that I had been familiar with those texts for a good many years before I began my theological studies. These extended, with various gaps, from 1957 until my ordination in 1964. That was a period when people were beginning to make use of newer translations, and the ones which I remember in particular as being useful and helpful were the Revised Standard Version and the work of J.B. Phillips – in particular the *Letters to Young Churches*, which came as a revelation to anyone who had wrestled with the obscurities of the Epistles in the King James Bible.

I have since wondered about the effects brought on by long contact with the Authorised Version and The Book of Common Prayer – an experience which it is difficult for younger Christians to imagine, whether they are younger in years or in membership of the Church. There have been so many modern translations, now in use over so many years, that almost everybody has become familiar with hearing and reading the Bible in a translation which is reasonably accessible, comprehensible, even down-to-earth. We do, however, need to remember that a Bible Society survey which took place in the mid-1980s revealed a significant number of people who still had contact only with the Authorised Version. Of those who were questioned about which version of the Bible they had last referred to, 34 per cent said that it had been the Authorised Version, while in the south-west of England (where I have spent most of my ministry) the figure was 46 per cent.

One of my practices as a diocesan bishop is to try to visit confirmation candidates on a separate occasion some time before the confirmation itself, so that I have a chance to meet them and talk to them in a way which is not possible after the service. I am able to ask them about their familiarity with the Bible, and about the version which they have themselves, and it is still not at all uncommon to find that young people have access only to the Authorised Version, or that some fond godparent is planning to give them a white leather-bound copy in minute type and still in the wonderful English of 1611.

But to return to the question: What is the effect of being exposed to the Authorised Version? I suspect that it can result in one of three reactions: the first may be above all incomprehension, followed by irritation and rejection. The second may be fascination with what seems mysterious, with the resonant beauty of the language which conveys something of the importance, the otherness and the authority of the Bible. Folk religion, particularly in rural areas, is still being fed in this way, by memories of, or current exposure to, worship in which The Book of Common Prayer and the Authorised Version are regularly used. There is in this a valuable element of poetry, the effect of language which is on the borderline of comprehensibility. You do not have to *understand* something in order to be helped by it, edified or nurtured by it, otherwise there would be no place for poetry in people's lives. It can be claimed to be one of the positive virtues of the Authorised Version, as of The Book of Common Prayer, that it is not readily comprehensible. This reminds me of the reported words of an Irish Christian, expressing her dissatisfaction with the new Mass in English: 'It no longer means so much', she said, 'now that I understand it.' This is perhaps a characteristically Irish statement, but it contains within it an important truth. There are different dimensions of meaning, and the increased intelligibility of the new service lacks the elements of mystery and transcendence which almost everyone recognises in the old. We need to bear this particular element in mind, although also to keep it in its place, when we consider modern translations.

The third possible reaction, more likely from an intelligent and enquiring person than from someone with relatively little education, is to be stimulated by the sheer difficulty of the Authorised Version text to look more deeply into it. I think that this sometimes happened in the old days in school work on the Bible, and I recall in particular an RE lesson when a passage of Ephesians came to life as we wrestled with what it really meant in contemporary English. I have never since that day forgotten how vivid and powerful are St Paul's words about 'letting not the sun go down on your wrath'.

I hope that these details of personal experience are not entirely irrelevant, because I believe that any individual's reaction to the Bible, and use of it, are to some extent influenced by the history of his or her personal experience. I mentioned that in my student days I relied quite heavily on the Revised Standard Version and J. B. Phillips' translation, the former for study and the latter for personal, devotional use. In retrospect, the choice was significant in ways which I certainly did not realise at the time. For those two translations are good examples of the opposite ends of the spectrum in terms of the translator's task. I believe that it is worth devoting some time to this important question of principle. What is the translator driving at? What method is he using? We need to bear these questions in mind in any consideration of different versions, and in deciding which version is appropriate to use for a particular purpose.

I must apologise to those who are already familiar with this next point, but my guess is that most committed Christians, even regular churchgoers and Bible readers, have not in fact actually thought about it in a direct and conscious way, although we are all of us, of course, at least subconsciously aware of the issue. I am referring here to the question of whether a translation of the Bible which aims at accuracy is going to use the method of 'formal correspondence', that is, that the English words should as far as possible be the equivalent of the Hebrew or the Greek: or of 'dynamic equivalence', or 'dynamic transference', that is, that the modern translation conveys as nearly as possible, as far as our knowledge of language, culture and idiom allows, what the original would have meant in its original setting. The translator may set out with the view that formal correspondence is what he is aiming at, or he may consciously reject that method of translation in favour of dynamic equivalence. Or he may decide that what he needs to achieve is some kind of compromise between the two.

Let me give an example: the story of Elijah and the Prophets of Baal, in 1 Kings 18.21. Elijah is challenging the people to decide between God and Baal. In the Authorised Version he says, 'How long halt ye between two opinions?' In the Good News Bible he says, 'How much longer will it take you to make up your minds?' The literal meaning of the Hebrew, that is to say in terms of formal correspondence, is 'How long will you go on limping on two divided things?' It can be claimed with some conviction that the 'divided things' were legs, so that as well as asking his question, Elijah was phrasing it in a way which mocked the strange dances of the prophets of Baal. In this case, the indication is that we really need to find a translation which will be dynamically equivalent, rather than formally correspondent. But is there any phrase in English which manages to convey a sense of mockery, the play on the dance, and also Elijah's challenge? There is an ingenious translation in the Bengali Bible, which makes Elijah say, 'How long will you remain with your feet in two boats?' People in Bangladesh are always coming and going between long dugout boats tied up next to each other in the river, and anyone who has found himself with one foot in one boat and one in another and the gap growing wider will have a good idea of what the translator is trying to convey. There's a challenge for the next English translation . . .

This issue of whether translators should aim at formal correspondence or dynamic equivalence is by no means a new one. As long ago as the sixteenth century, Luther, who was an expert on Bible translation in his day, and whose translation still forms the basis of the Standard German Bible which is in regular use throughout the world, said, 'Whoever would speak German must not use Hebrew style. Rather, he must see to it, once he understands the Hebrew author, that he concentrates on the sense of text, asking himself what the Germans say in such a situation.' It may not be a new problem, but it remains a very live issue for Bible translators. How far is paraphrase legitimate or helpful? For academic study, and especially for comparison with the original language, the answer is, not at all; hence the continuing usefulness and high reputation of the Revised Standard Version and, to a lesser extent, of the more recent New International Version.

But there are reasons for preferring a paraphrastic translation, in which case great care has to be taken, not only to make sure that the idiom used in the new language is a convincing and effective one, but also that neither the idiom nor any incidental detail is likely to date very rapidly. Take, for example, Mark 6.37: in the original Greek, the disciples complained that it would cost 200 denarii to buy enough bread to feed the people. The Revised Standard Version, with its formal correspondence style of translation, simply renders this into English. The Good News Bible makes it '200 silver coins'. But what does it actually mean? How much is it in real terms? The New English Bible, trying to be helpful and to put modern value on it, says that it would cost at least £20 to buy enough food. But the New English Bible was published in 1961, after a period of translation which had lasted since 1946. Even if we assume that £20 was calculated in 1961, we all know what has happened to inflation since then. The New International Version has tried to overcome this particular problem of detail by making the disciples say, 'That would take eight months of a man's wages' — not exactly a colloquial phrase that one can imagine coming from the lips of the disciples in the circumstances, but at least a phrase which means something in terms of value. That is only one of the very many illustrations of how difficult and complicated it may be to find a satisfactory, dynamically equivalent translation.

To sum up this section, formal correspondence is word–for–word translation; dynamic equivalence is meaning–for–meaning translation. Each can be said to be accurate, although they use different techniques to achieve the desired result.

Let us now look at the factors which have been at work in encouraging the appearance of ever more new translations. It has been calculated that in the twentieth century alone there have been at least seventy-five new translations in the English language. For this prodigious output there must be some good reasons.

The first is, of course, that new evidence constantly comes to light to update the textual material on the basis of which previous translations were made. The translators in the seventeenth century had access to very defective original documents, and the progress that has been made since then has been enormous. That progress continues, although of course very much more slowly.

The second reason for wanting a new translation is the way in which language changes. Many of the words in the Authorised Version are completely incomprehensible nowadays, whereas others have changed their meaning so dramatically that it requires a dictionary to know what the original text actually means. For example, 'conversation' in the seventeenth century is the equivalent of today's word 'lifestyle'; 'prevent' in the language of the Authorised Version simply means 'go before', while 'chambering' would have to be translated in a paraphrastic modern translation as 'sleeping around'. The danger in trying to find an appropriate modern word is that language is still changing, and much more rapidly now than in the past. This means that translations which attempt to achieve a kind of contemporary colloquial vigour are in grave danger of being rapidly outdated. There is also a wide variety of cultural practice; I remember vividly the story from Bishop Hensley Henson's *Retrospect of an Unimportant Life*[1] in which he recalls the agitation which took place in his lifetime over the use of the word 'indifferently' to mean 'impartially'. Hensley Henson claimed that whereas 'impartial' was a word understood only by educated people, everyone knew what 'indifferently' meant, at least in the sense in which it appears in The Book of Common Prayer. He asked his gardener 'What is the meaning of impartially?' 'I don't know,' replied the man. 'What is the meaning of indifferently?', asked Hensley Henson. 'Ah', said the man, 'that means not making any difference.'

The third factor which governs the decision about making a new translation, and the form which it should take, is the purpose for which it is intended. Who is going to read the new translation? Is it to be used for purposes of study, or for public worship, or for personal devotion and private reading? Is it for an educated, literate audience? Or is it to achieve the widest possible acceptability? The answers to these questions will dictate the size of the vocabulary to be used, and the literary style.

There is a particularly notable contrast to be drawn between the New English Bible and the Good News Bible. The New English Bible is celebrated (or notorious) for its occasional use of extremely rare words, and the basic presumption which seems to lie behind it that its readers will be able to cope with its literary language; 'He prostrated himself in obeisance' is not common language. Sometimes one feels that there has been a misguided search for grandeur of language for its own sake, as in the appalling 'effulgence of his splendour' for the Authorised Version's 'the brightness of his glory' (Hebrews 1.3), a disastrous mistake which has mercifully been put right in the Revised English Bible. It is the use of common language (but note that is by no means the same thing as basic English) which makes the Good News Bible so deservedly popular, and which also means that the Living Bible has an appeal in certain circles.

The fourth factor which may dictate changes in a new translation is a desire to achieve ecumenical agreement. Generally speaking, of course, it is highly desirable that a translation should be able to achieve the widest possible circulation, but it may be that an existing translation, when it is adapted to make it acceptable to another Christian tradition, in fact changes for the worse. The Revised Standard Version was published in 1952, as an American Protestant achievement. Negotiations took place with the Roman Catholic authorities to see whether a text could be produced which would be acceptable also to them, and in 1973 the Common Bible appeared – the Revised Standard Version with changes which made it possible for the Roman Catholic Church to authorise its use. Unfortunately this involved retrograde alterations from the point of view of accuracy. The longer ending of Mark, which in the original Revised Standard Version had been printed in italics, as a quite obviously separate, less authoritative part of the text, is reinstated in a way which makes it appear to be a legitimate alternative to the abrupt ending at chapter 16, verse 8.

So we turn to the question of which is the best translation for any particular purpose. Inevitably, there will be an element of subjective choice about anything which is said on this subject. There is always the need to bear in mind the specific purpose for which a translation is needed; I have already referred to the continuing popularity of the Revised Standard Version for study purposes, and I have implied that I myself prefer to use the Good News Bible in working with young people. But there is always going to be a serious objection on one ground or another. Although I am in general satisfied with the Good News Bible as a vigorous, reasonably accurate and thoroughly accessible version, it is seriously let down by one or two disastrous mistakes. The most notorious of these is the translation of what the Authorised Version calls 'the flesh' by the phrase 'our human nature' (as in Romans 8). This is to make a very sweeping judgement about human nature, and the very much to be preferred translation of the New English Bible, 'our lower nature' seems to me to be much nearer the truth. But what is one to do? Not give the Good News Bible to young people because one disapproves of that particular disastrous mistake? Or give it to them, and when the opportunity arises, point out the fault which is there in the Good News version?

If we look in detail at a number of translations and attempt to compare them by looking at the way in which they handle particularly difficult passages, I think this will become even clearer. The passages which I have in mind are three: John 2.4, in the story of the wedding at Cana in Galilee, where Jesus responds to his mother's prompting; Romans 13.10b, in which Paul sums up his teaching on love and law; and the way in which the longer ending of Mark is handled.

Let us look first at that extremely difficult verse from John 2.4. How one wishes that one had been a fly on the wall as the panels of translators discussed and argued together about what to do about it. In the Greek it is very abrupt, it sounds discourteous and it strikes a thoroughly jarring note. There are just five words, of which the literal translation is: 'What to you and to me, woman?' This seems remarkably harsh and dismissive. The evidence seems to be that the Greek word which is translated literally 'woman' does not in fact have the almost insulting sense which is would have in English; it can convey some sense of affection. And yet it has somehow seemed unthinkable that our Lord could address his mother in this way. There is so little trace of kindness or consideration or affection – or even courtesy – let alone a sympathetic view of the embarrassing crisis which has blown up in the course of the wedding party. No wonder modern translators have wondered what to do with these five words, and have resisted using a formal correspondence version.

The Authorised Version plunges straight in: 'Woman, what have I to do with thee?' The Revised Standard Version remains close, but reverses the order: 'O woman, what have you to do with me?' But the New Revised Standard Version can no longer bear not to soften the words, and gives us 'Woman, what concern is that to you and to me?' – avoiding the implicit personal antagonism of the original, and by implication drawing Jesus closer to his mother by focusing on a problem which does not directly concern either of them. J.B. Phillips picks up this interpretation: 'Is that your concern or mine, mother?' further softening and paraphrasing, in a way unjustified by the text. The Jerusalem Bible, 'Woman, why turn to me?' keeps it fairly harsh, and so in a different – but perhaps not unfair – paraphrase, does the Good News Bible: 'You must not tell me what to do.' But it leaves out the word 'woman'. The New English Bible has 'Your concern, mother, is not mine.' But this is altered in the Revised English Bible – the new version of the New English Bible – to 'That is no concern of mine.' 'Mother' is left out, but the translators could not cope with 'woman'. The New International Version, which claims some degree of formal correspondence, is wildly wrong here with 'Dear woman, why do you involve me?' – thus introducing two quite unfounded paraphrastic additions. The Living Bible is even worse, with its 'I can't help you now' – introducing yet another completely new, and totally unjustified, implication that Jesus *will* help later. Of course we know that he did, but to read the subsequent action back into the original response is not only textually completely wrong, but it seriously undermines and devalues his mother's unruffled, trusting words, 'Do what he tells you.' The two most extraordinary versions of these words which I have come across – and I promise not to use these translations again – are from the old Weymouth translation of 1903, which claimed to be based on the original Greek, but offers us the bizarre translation, 'Leave it to me'; and there is the long-forgotten E.V. Rieu translation, which makes Jesus sound like a New York cop: 'Lady, why bring your troubles to me?'

So there we are. There is an amazing range of ways of tackling this extraordinarily difficult phrase, and I share them with you to show the range of ways in which translators have tried either to do straightforward justice to the text, or to find some way of interpreting it that seems to be consistent with our other knowledge of Jesus' words and ways, and also with the expectations and susceptibilities of modern readers; we can see the extremes of imaginative dynamic equivalence to which some will go. I have already revealed my general preference for the Revised Standard Version and the Good News Bible, and both come out quite well from this particular exercise, the John 2.4 test. The Revised Standard Version's 'Woman, what have you to do with me?' is pretty accurate and uncompromising; while of the attempts at dynamic equivalence, the Good News' 'You must not tell me what to do', although it evades the issue of the word 'woman', does have something of the right kind of harshness about it to reflect what is there in the Greek.

Romans 13.10b, raises a different issue, and a serious theological one. Paul has been discussing the relationship of the Christian gospel to the Jewish Law, and affirming the primacy of love as the determining factor in Christian living. The chapter starts with the well-known exhortation to obey the civil authorities as having some divine authority behind them; then comes a reference to the Torah, and to the commandments embodied in the Jewish Law, both prohibitions and demands. So by verse 10 he has in mind a wide range of human activity – personal and corporate, civic and religious – and is making the point that love alone is the basis of all these aspects of life for a Christian. Literally the Greek means love is law's 'fulfilment'; the Authorised Version quite legitimately interprets it as 'fulfilling' – the action, the fact of putting love into action, rather than the finished event, the fulfilment. So the Authorised Version seems perfectly acceptable when it says, 'Love is the fulfilling of the law.' The Revised Standard Version retains the identical wording: the New English Bible and the New International Version opt for 'fulfilment' rather than 'fulfilling'. The Living Bible, the dynamic equivalence translation *par excellence*, is very long-winded indeed; it is a brave effort and only partly successful: 'That is why love fully satisfies all of God's requirements. It is the only law you need.' This is one place at which the Good News Bible gets a very black mark indeed, with its version, 'To love, then, is to obey the whole Law.' You can see why they put it like that, but the real risk is that readers – or listeners – will get hold of an entirely wrong idea, and come away with a preoccupation with obedience, almost the exact opposite of the freedom from being under the Law that St Paul is constantly affirming; and it is made worse in the Good News Bible by the fact that the word 'Law' has a capital 'L', i.e. 'to love *is to obey the whole of the Jewish Law* (Torah)'. Oh dear!

It is interesting to see how the Protestant Living Bible's 'That's why love satisfies all of God's requirements. It's the only law you need' is quite close to the Roman Catholic Jerusalem Bible, which has 'That is why love is the answer to every one of the Commandments.' Both these versions are too restrictive, and introduce the idea of satisfaction or answer, both of which imply for me a kind of scoring process, which is both alien in character to Paul's thought, and also too sweeping in its implied superseding of the Law. This is a point at which the New Jerusalem Bible makes quite a radical change, and goes back to a more traditional, more formally correspondent version, which is in fact more accurate: 'So love is the fulfilment of the Law.'

Finally, because once again it raises a different issue, let us look very briefly at the longer ending of Mark (chapter 16). The fact that it is printed as part of the Gospel in the Authorised Version is hardly surprising, in view of the state of textual knowledge in the early seventeenth century. But the ways in which modern translators handle it are surprisingly varied. We have already noted its reinstatement for denominational reasons in the Common Bible (the ecumenical and especially Roman Catholic version of the Revised Standard Version). The original Revised Standard Version is really the most satisfactory, since it prints verses 9ff in small italics, distinguishing them very clearly from verses 1 to 8. The New English Bible and the Revised English Bible print both the short and the long alternative endings, with suitable and satisfactory explanatory notes about their status; J. B. Phillips calls the longer ending 'an ancient appendix', the New International Version prints it out, but indicates that it is an unreliable text; the Good News Bible has bold headings in capital letters 'An old ending to the Gospel' and 'Another old ending'. It is the Living Bible and the Jerusalem Bible which are the most misleading; the Living Bible says, 'Not found in the original manuscripts but may be considered an appendix giving additional facts' (facts indeed: more like a farrago of mythological nonsense). The Jerusalem Bible admits that the longer ending may not have been written by Mark, 'though it is old enough' – which is not helpful and not even true.

To return to the question of which translation is best, is to return to the increasing certainty that none can be singled out for particular virtue or particular suitability. It entirely depends on what you want a translation for, and who is going to be reading or listening to it. If I may be entirely personal here, I will share with you my own practice and my own preference. I still love the Authorised Version, and I believe that it has an important part to play in the life of the Church. Where the Holy Communion Service is still celebrated according to The Book of Common Prayer I use the readings from the Prayer Book in the Authorised Version, unless there is some overwhelming reason why one of them needs to be read in another translation in order to be understandable. I vividly remember my days as a school chaplain, when I was at my most radical, and wanting to introduce new forms of service and new translations at every possible opportunity; it was when Series Three first came out and I fell upon it with great delight. Another chaplain was appointed who was a traditionalist compared with me, and we had long discussions about what we should do at the early Communion service according to The Book of Common Prayer. He stoutly affirmed that if the Authorised Version were read with real intelligence and sympathy, it could practically always be made comprehensible; I doubted him at the time, but I have since come to agree entirely with what he said. I believe that those people who find it helpful to worship in archaic language (and this raises whole issues as to what the justification for that particular conviction is, into which I will not go here), on the whole prefer consistency. I find it personally very irritating when those leading worship jump from one form of language to another, even for example not bothering to use the Rite B form of the Collects when celebrating a Rite B Eucharist. So I believe that consistency of style is something that matters, although I also believe that there may be some circumstances in which, provided the reason is made plain, it is possible to mix styles to good effect.

But I find myself very slowly moving away from this fondness for the Authorised Version. When I go to a village church for a Harvest Festival service, for example, and find that the lessons are being read from the Authorised Version, I am not always exactly delighted, and I am beginning to feel the same about the traditional service of Nine Lessons and Carols. Perhaps this is a particular difficulty for a bishop, who has no rooted place of worship, but finds himself somewhere different every Sunday. It is difficult to know what translation is going to be used; and to prepare a sermon using a text from one version, and then to find that whoever is reading the lessons has, on the spur of the moment, chosen another, can be quite disconcerting.

I have to admit to a degree of concern about this waning enthusiasm for the Authorised Version which I have recognised in myself, because I am convinced that we need to retain the

Authorised Version. It is an extremely important part of our culture, it is a uniquely beautiful expression of the Word of God, and it has a very significant place within the culture of English-speaking peoples altogether. It has contributed an enormous amount to literature in the English language, and decreasing familiarity with the Authorised Version is bound to bring with it a decreasing ability to appreciate some of the subtleties and nuances of English literature. I quote a paragraph from the admirable address given in 1990 by Professor Basil Mitchell to the Prayer Book Society:

The case for retaining the older books is simple and, I believe, unanswerable. They were written at a time when the English language was at its most flexible, most expressive and most resonant. They have left their mark upon the English language and English literature ever since in such a manner that no one could seriously study either without becoming familiar with them. They are deeply intertwined with our musical tradition and they are peculiarly well suited to being spoken aloud. They resemble the scriptures and liturgies of many religions in being composed in a style which was somewhat archaic even at the time of writing, giving them a certain 'timeless' quality. They are not, of course, and could not be literally timeless, but being of another time and having endured the test of time, they transcend to some degree 'the changes and chances of this mortal life'. Above all, they are, quite incontestably, great literature. It is sometimes argued that the literary quality of the works is irrelevant to their use in Christian worship and that the splendour of the language may even distract the worshipper from the plain meaning of the text. But it cannot be insisted too strongly that the power of great literature is not a matter of ornament and embellishment but of using words most effectively to convey the full meaning of what is said. There are modes of communication in which surface meaning is all that counts, but this is not the case with poetry or any writing in which the whole person is seriously engaged.[2]

I believe that the Revised Standard Version is still an excellent compromise. It is reasonably accurate in textual terms, it retains the predominantly formal correspondence style of translation, and in this way it very often echoes the Authorised Version. It is significant that in The Alternative Service Book, the readings which it is expected people will remember from the Authorised Version, and to which they will be attached in the Authorised Version, are always printed from the Revised Standard Version – simply because it remains close to the Authorised Version in terms of shape and cadence. The New English Bible has turned out to be a very satisfactory modern language version for public worship, although it was not designed for that purpose. There are some strange lapses in it, and for that reason people tend to prefer the New International Version.

My own experience of the New International Version is that, although in theory I approve of it, and I believe that it is a reasonable compromise between formal correspondence and occasional essays into dynamic equivalence, it is not a satisfactory version to which to listen. I base this conclusion on several months' experience in the cathedral at Hereford, where it has recently come into use for the weekday services. The Chapter are beginning to agree with my convictions, I believe, and I have noticed that some canons tend to use the Revised Standard Version once more. I am sure, though, that for young people the Good News Bible is the best choice, despite its occasional serious mistakes in terms of translation and interpretation. But its vigour, its limited vocabulary, the clear way in which the sections of texts are divided up with headings which make the thrust of a book easy to follow, its brilliant line drawings by Annie Vallotton, as well as the helpful introductions at the beginning of each book, all combine to make this the Bible which is the most user-friendly of all. The Living Bible, which I suppose in theory might be regarded as a rival to the Good News Bible, I find very distasteful indeed. It is very American, it is very long-winded, frequently inaccurate, and it betrays its middle-class American origins only too clearly.

The Jerusalem Bible is in some ways admirable, but it does have some serious lapses – some of which I have mentioned. I also find the Old Testament difficult to read, with the constant reiteration of Yahweh, in place of a more accessible name for God. This seems to me to be a bit of theological and linguistic pedantry which it is simply not appropriate to import into a Bible which is to be read aloud.

But it is not merely a question of which translation is the best for a given purpose. In order to understand the Bible, any informed Christian needs more information and more help than the text itself provides. This is why a Bible with some kind of annotation, some kind of brief commentary notes attached to it, and preferably printed on the same page as the text, is of enormous value if one is trying to understand what the Word of God truly is. Strangely enough, the Bible which I have found most helpful for my own use is the Ecumenical French translation, the Traduction Oecuménique de la Bible (TOB)[3]. I came across this as a result of several twinning experiences with French Roman Catholic dioceses and I have been interested to discover how widely used it is by Roman Catholics, although it is in fact a translation which originated in the French Reformed Church. Fortunately I can read the French well enough to use it, and I find that the notes are of exactly of the right scale and style to help me in my understanding of the text. There are occasional instances of clear denominational prejudice coming out in the notes, but there is a kind of even-handedness – in which alternative points of view are clearly set out – which makes this acceptable.

There is of course no substitute, for the serious student, for the original text itself. I am sad to say that I do not read Hebrew at all, and my Greek is fairly sketchy, but I can manage to read the Gospels in Greek, and I try to do so when I am saying the Office on my own. I try also to remember to take a Greek text with me if I know that I am going to a service at which I shall be listening to the New Testament. Even my very limited knowledge of Greek is enough to enable me to understand that not even the most skilful translation can convey quite the sense of the original. It is extraordinary how the quality of the original writing does come across in the Greek in a way which just cannot be captured in a translation.

I was involved in an interesting and entertaining exchange based on a Greek text when I was at the Conference of European Churches in Prague. Towards the end of the Assembly we were debating the official message which was going to be issued. It included a quotation from 2 Corinthians 5.17. In the first version of the message the translation used was, 'So if anyone is in Christ, there is a new creation: the old thing has passed away, see, everything has become new.' Quite apart from the peculiar and unhappy use of 'the old thing', the text was attacked by a Greek professor. He pointed out that it was very bad English, and that it really ought to be re-written. It is not a case, he said, of the text saying, 'If anyone is in Christ'; the text says, 'when anyone is in Christ', and goes on to say, 'he is a new creature'. I joined in the debate, pointing out that it was not simply that it was bad English, but that the Greek text is in fact unclear. In the Greek there are six words, which translate literally as: 'If anyone in Christ new creation (or new creature)'. The Greek manuscripts tend to agree that it is the word 'if', not the word 'when'; but most modern translations show that there are several ways of translating this particular sentence. I happened to have with me a copy of the New English Bible, which sets this out very clearly in its footnotes, and I was able to read various possible translations, and say that the Committee should look again at the whole matter.

During the coffee break, the Greek professor buttonholed me and argued that really I was quite wrong about this. Luckily one of the other Church of England representatives, a very intelligent laywoman, had her Greek Testament with her, so for ten minutes or so there was a tremendous argument outside the conference hall as we Anglicans argued with the Greek about the Greek text. I am glad to say that in the end we won, and he had to agree that we were right. So it does come in handy from time to time to know just enough of the Greek to be able to argue with the Greeks. I only wish that I could do the same with the Hebrew.

I have been very impressed, in my contacts with those involved in theological education in Germany and in Holland, to discover just how rigorous the linguistic teaching has to be for someone who wishes to be ordained. In both those countries (and I refer here to the Lutheran and Reformed Churches), students spend two years doing language studies before they embark on theology itself. They are required to be proficient in Hebrew, Greek and Latin – something which makes our theological education look very basic indeed. I am not quite sure about the Latin, and when I questioned a German friend about that he was at a loss to account for it, except to say that it was traditional. But that does underline for me the importance of making sure that as many people as possible have some familiarity with the original text, particularly if they are going to be involved in preaching and teaching.

The answer to the question of which translation one should use is clearly that one has to use many. I think we need to be very grateful to the Alternative Service Book for having ranged across a number of translations, and given us in the printed readings Sunday by Sunday an experience of a number of different translations to set alongside the Authorised Version. I do not necessarily agree in each case with the choice which is made in the Alternative Service Book, but I understand the principles which lie behind the decision not to be limited to one particular translation. I believe that no serious, thoughtful Christian should rely on one translation and ignore the others. We need to be deeply grateful for the enormous amount of scholarship, energy, imagination and care that has gone into the process of translation, particularly during this century. We are privileged in having access to a range of translations unparalleled in human history. It can sometimes be bewildering, but it is also deeply enriching.

Notes

1   DIVINE REVELATION THROUGH HUMAN EXPERIENCE

 1 Robert Young, *Analytical Concordance to the Bible* (James Clarke 1879; Lutterworth Press 1989).   Edward Robinson, *Greek and English Lexicon of the New Testament* (1836).

2   'THE BEGINNING OF THE GOSPEL IS NOTHING BUT THE WHOLE OLD TESTAMENT'

 1 See, for example, C.H. Dodd, *According to the Scriptures*, (London 1952).
 2 E.g., B.S. Childs, *Introduction to the Old Testament as Scripture* (London 1979).

3   WHO IS REALLY IN CHARGE – BIBLE OR CHURCH?

 1 Peter Selby, *BeLonging: Challenge to a Tribal Church* (SPCK 1991), p.4.
 2 J.I. Packer, *Fundamentalism and the Word of God* (IVP 1958).   John A.T. Robinson, *Honest to God* (SCM Press 1963).
 3 J.S. Spong, *Rescuing the Bible from Fundamentalism* (Harper 1991), p.247.
 4 Peter Selby, *Look for the Living: the Corporate Nature of Resurrection Faith* (SCM Press 1976).
 5 See, e.g., Anthony C. Thiselton, *New Horizons in Hermeneutic* (Marshall Pickering 1992).
 6 Gabriel Josipovici, *The Book of God* (Yale University Press 1988), p.302.
 7 S.M. Schneiders, *The Revelatory Text* (Harper 1991), p.59.
 8 ibid., p.66.
 9 Graham Shaw, *The Cost of Authority* (SCM Press 1983), p.274.
10 Schneiders, op.cit., ch. 7, an investigation of John 4.1–42.
11 R.S. Sugirtharajah (ed.), *Voices from the Margin* (SPCK 1991).
12 ibid., p.2.
13 This is the kind of enterprise which Christopher Rowland described in his inaugural lecture as Dean Ireland's Professor of Biblical Exegesis at

Oxford University, under the title 'Open Thy Mouth for the Dumb', May 1992.

14 Jürgen Moltmann, *The Church in the Power of the Spirit* (Harper 1991), pp.126–130.

15 Schneiders, op.cit., p.66.

5 PRAYER AND THE SCRIPTURES

Bible references are from the Revised Standard Version. Revised English Bible and New International Version.

1 Vatican II, *Dogmatic Constitution on Divine Revelation*, Chapter 6, v.1.21.

2 André Louf, *Teach Us to Pray: Learning A Little About Prayer* (Darton, Longman & Todd 1974).

3 Thomas Merton, *Bread in the Wilderness* (Burns & Oates 1976), p.80.

4 *Celebrating Common Prayer: A Version of the Daily Office SSF*, (Mowbray/Cassell 1992), p.viii.

5 ibid., p.563.

6 THE LITURGICAL USE OF SCRIPTURE

Quotations from the Psalms are from the Coverdale version in The Book of Common Prayer. Other Bible quotations are mainly from the New English Bible.

1 Charles Williams, 'Apologue on the Parable of the Wedding Guest', pub. *Time and Tide*, Dec. 1940, quoted in J.V. Taylor, *The Christ-like God* (SCM Press, 1992).

2 *Auguries of Innocence*, 53, by William Blake (1757–1827).

3 Verse 2 of 'The God of Abraham Praise' by T. Olivers (1725–1799), based on the Hebrew Yigdal.

4 *Hymn of the Nativity* 1.79, by Richard Crashaw (1612?–1649).

5 *Celebrating Common Prayer: A Version of the Daily Office SSF*, (Mowbray/Cassell 1992).

6 *Far from the Madding Crowd* (1874) by Thomas Hardy (1840–1928).

7 The Alternative Service Book 1980, p.11. Copyright © The Central Board of Finance of the Church of England.

7 PREACHING FROM A TEXT

1 Hugh Montefiore, *Preaching for our Planet* (Mowbray/Cassell, 1992). Bible references are mainly from the Authorised Version.
2 Gerhard von Rad, *Genesis* (SCM Press rev. ed. 1979).

8 A VARIETY OF VERSIONS

Quotations from the Psalms are from the Coverdale version in The Book of Common Prayer.

1 *Retrospect of an Unimportant Life* (3 vols, 1942–50) by Herbert Hensley Henson (1863–1947).
2 Basil Mitchell, *Multiculturalism and the Prayer Book*, delivered to the Prayer Book Society in Leicester (September 1990).
3 Traduction Oecuménique de la Bible (Editions du Cerf 1975).